**more**

gluten-free *and easy*
recipes

Published by Sellers Publishing, Inc.
Copyright © 2017 Sellers Publishing, Inc.
Copyright text © 2017 Robyn Russell
Copyright photography © 2017 Elizabeth Ginn
All rights reserved.
First published in 2008 by Murdoch Books

Cover design: Charlotte Cromwell
Design concept: Tania Simanowsky
Interior Designer: Heather Menzies
Project manager: Desney Shoemark
Editor: Kim Rowney
Production: Kita George
Photographer: Elizabeth Ginn
Stylists: Robyn Russell and Elizabeth Ginn

Sellers Publishing, Inc.
161 John Roberts Road, South Portland, Maine 04106
Visit our Web site: sellerspublishing.com
E-mail: rsp@rsvp.com

ISBN 13: 978-1-4162-4608-4
Library of Congress Control Number: 2016946053

10 9 8 7 6 5 4 3 2 1

Printed and bound in China

more gluten-free *and easy* recipes

Enjoy more of your favorite foods with these 90+ recipes

Robyn Russell

SELLERS
PUBLISHING

Contents

Introduction

It's funny the path life takes. Here I am writing the introduction to my second gluten-free cookbook, yet it doesn't seem that long ago that I was blissfully ignorant of the whole celiac condition and I'd never heard the term "gluten free." It was back in the early 1980s, as a brand-new Ansett flight attendant, that I handed a passenger a special meal, tightly wrapped in plastic, with a bright green "Gluten Free" sticker on top. I asked the gentleman what was gluten and why was it free? He explained to me about celiac disease and listed all the foods he couldn't eat, and I clearly remember thinking that I may as well just give him the little plastic tray to chew on.

Ten years later and those thoughts came rushing back as I was sitting in the gastroenterologist's office being told that I had celiac disease and would need to exclude wheat, barley, oats and rye from my diet for the rest of my life. "Off you go," the doctor said. "Stick with the diet and you'll be as good as new in no time." I headed home in a state of shock, wondering what on earth I was going to eat.

At least it was better than the doctor before him who'd told me it was all in my head: Finally I knew what was wrong, that, in fact, something really had been wrong and it wasn't just nerves or anxiety. I had a medically diagnosed condition with a name and I was relieved to know decisively what I was dealing with. At last I could get on with my life.

First things first and I diligently inspected every item in my pantry. Apart from throwing out the obvious no-no's such as rye crispbread and wheat-laden breakfast cereals, I was staggered to discover how much gluten I'd been ingesting from the most unlikely sources. Even my rice crackers didn't pass muster as I'd always bought the brand with a soy sauce that was made from wheat. Being left with a few cans of tuna and a bag of rice, my next stop was the supermarket. Up and down the aisles I went, reading every ingredient panel and rejecting so much that despite being in the store for hours I could still proceed through the 12 items or less checkout! Things are much better these days with the expanded health food section in larger supermarkets and even some dedicated gluten-free sections, but at that time it was very slim pickings indeed.

Luckily for me in those dark days after first being diagnosed my body told me exactly what it needed, and I craved meat, eggs, vegetables and fruit. Over time, finding quality ingredients and providing myself with nourishing meals turned into a love of cooking that has now grown into an exciting new career. Every cloud has a silver lining as they say, but for me a positive outlook and a determination not to accept any impingement on my lifestyle has been equally as important as my diet. I also refuse to be classified as a "celiac sufferer." Sure I'm a celiac, but I'm not suffering at all. I am also not diseased, which sounds like I might be contagious, and how I wish someone would change the name to something that more accurately describes an annoying condition that is very well managed with a gluten-free diet.

So apart from my personal gripe about terminology, life is pretty good. Currently I'm the only celiac in our little household, but with its strong genetic link and celiac disease on both sides of the family I'm watching my daughter like a hawk. Strangely, our dog has been on gluten-free dog biscuits for years since the vet recommended it as a treatment for itchy puppy skin and I must say at 13 years old his coat is still shiny and thick!

I consider myself fluent in "celiac speak" these days and am confident I can deal with tricky situations when they arise, or maybe after all this time I've just trained my family and friends pretty well. But if you've recently been diagnosed with celiac disease and the whole gluten-free thing seems totally overwhelming here are a few pointers from a "been there, done that" celiac.

* This is not a "take a pill and get on with it" condition. Chances are you've been unwell for a while, so be gentle with yourself and allow plenty of time to recover — it can take months to feel truly well again.
* Consider joining a celiac support group in your area. They will likely have all the latest information and offer a wonderful support network.
* Some people will think this is just a passing phase and that next week you'll be on The Grapefruit Diet. Try to be patient and polite.
* Learn how to read food labels; you might be surprised at how much processed food you can still eat.
* Get a referral from your doctor for a bone density scan. Long term undiagnosed celiac disease can lead to osteoporosis.
* Friends and relatives are well meaning but don't always have the best advice. Find a professional health care worker with a good understanding of celiac disease and manage your health with their assistance.
* You will find it hard to be as spontaneous as you used to be and will need to plan meals ahead. Think about using leftovers for lunch and use your freezer more. Travelling will require a whole new degree of organization.
* Be aware of contamination. You can't just scrape off the gluten or eat around it, and be careful of anything that is labelled gluten free but isn't packaged or stored separately from regular products.
* You never stop missing really good bread. Sorry, but there it is.

With our restricted diets celiacs can sometimes feel like second-class citizens, but you'll find plenty of ideas in this book to help you take charge and renew your enthusiasm for good food. You don't need to be a culinary school graduate to attempt any of my recipes and you'll find all of the ingredients at the supermarket or health food store. Now there's no need to accept mediocre when fabulous is right here at your fingertips. RR

A word of warning

Many packaged and processed ingredients and foods may contain gluten. You should always check the ingredient label on any commercial product that you intend to eat to be certain that gluten isn't lurking somewhere deep within an ingredients list. As awareness of celiac disease and gluten intolerance increases, the number of gluten-free products on the market continues to expand. While this makes your job of locating safe products in your local grocery store much easier, it is always best to double check those ingredient lists carefully.

This is not a medical book. If you suspect you may have an intolerance to gluten ask someone you know with celiac disease to recommend a local doctor who is familiar with the latest research and testing methods and book a professional consultation. It is strongly recommended that you don't commence a gluten-free diet before testing, as this can interfere with the accuracy of the results. RR

Bold font indicates a recipe is included in this book.

Tips for gluten-free baking

Listed below are a few baking tips that I've learned along the way:

✴ There is a dramatic difference between brands of white rice flour. Look for brands that are very fine and light, as opposed to some brands that aren't much better than sand, and result in gritty, heavy baked goods.

✴ Potato starch is often labelled potato flour though technically they're not the same product. Potato flour looks like ground up instant potatoes and has a grubby color, whereas potato starch (the one you want to use) is snowy white and has a very fine texture.

✴ Xanthan gum is used to prevent crumbling and helps keep baked goods moist. It works very well but some brands tend to be much stronger than others, so if you find your batter looks a little gluey, try using a bit less next time. Available from health food stores, xanthan gum is expensive but lasts for ages and a little goes a long way.

✴ Baking powder is added as a rising agent. Measure 1 cup of **Rice flour blend**, then replace 2 teaspoons of the flour with 2 teaspoons of baking powder to make 1 cup self-rising flour.

✴ In a few recipes I use sweet rice flour. Sometimes called glutinous rice flour, this refers to its sticky quality and does not imply it contains gluten. You'll find it in stores that sell Asian groceries.

✴ I like to add coconut oil to some of my baked goods, particularly biscuits, as it helps maintain a short, crisp texture. Look for virgin coconut oil in a jar at a health food store. Depending on the temperature it may be in a clear liquid form (above 77°F) or in an opaque solid form (below 77°F). Add to recipes in its liquid form, so scrape off as much as you need and stand that in a heatproof bowl in hot water — it melts quickly but doesn't heat the oil.

✴ I prefer to use bundt pans or ring molds if possible when baking cakes to avoid the dry outside and the undercooked middle that can happen when using regular cake pans. I'm a huge fan of silicone bakeware, especially for mini-cakes, pies, and tarts.

✴ Gluten-free baked goods seem to be particularly susceptible to high humidity, so choose recipes accordingly and try not to become discouraged.

Rice flour blend (gluten-free flour)

I'm staying with the **Rice flour blend** that I used in *Gluten Free and Easy* (my first book), as I think it bakes up better than any other flour blend I've tried. This flour is used in many of the recipes in this book, so it's a good idea to make it up in bulk so you've always got some on hand. It can be substituted cup for cup for wheat flour.

2 cups white rice flour
⅔ cup potato starch
⅓ cup tapioca flour

Mix all the ingredients thoroughly and store in an airtight container in the cupboard.

Be prepared

Stopping for takeout food because you don't feel like cooking just isn't an option when you are on a gluten-free diet, so a well-stocked pantry is vital and should provide all the essentials for a fast meal. With the basics in the cupboard and staples in the refrigerator, dinner can be ready in about 20 minutes, helping to avoid those bag-of-corn-chips-on-the-couch-in-front-of-the-television occasions.

In the cupboard

White rice flour
Brown rice flour
Rice flour blend (recipe page 9)
Soy flour
Potato starch
Tapioca flour
Cornstarch
Sweet rice flour
Quinoa flour

Confectioners' sugar
Superfine sugar
Brown sugar
Pure maple syrup
Golden syrup
Hazelnut spread
Baking powder
Baking soda
Xanthan gum
Unsweetened cocoa powder
Vanilla extract
Vanilla beans
Ground cinnamon
Whole nutmeg
Ground ginger
Cinnamon sticks

Papadums
Thin rice cakes
Rice crackers
Corn tortillas
Corn chips
Taco shells
Popcorn

Brown rice
Basmati rice
Wild blend rice
Arborio/risotto rice
Quinoa
Quinoa flakes
Polenta
Rice stick noodles, dried
Rice sheets, dried, round or square
Dried pasta
Coconut milk
Coconut cream

Tahini, hulled
Madras curry paste
Green curry paste

Crushed garlic, bottled
Grated ginger, bottled
Crushed chili, bottled
Tomato soup
Chopped tomatoes, canned
Tomato purée, canned
Tomato paste (concentrated purée)

Oyster sauce
Fish sauce
Soy sauce
Black olives
Roasted peppers, bottled
Marinated artichokes, bottled
Corn kernels, canned
Adzuki beans, canned
Cannellini beans, canned
Chickpeas, canned
Lentils, canned

Vegetable bouillon
Baby capers
Tuna in oil, canned
Red salmon, canned
Dijon mustard
Whole-grain mustard

Salsa, bottled
Apple slices, canned
Puréed apples and raspberries
Red wine vinegar
White wine vinegar
Cider vinegar
Olive oil
Canola oil
Macadamia oil
Coconut oil
Grapeseed oil

Puffed rice
Corn flakes
Rolled rice flakes
Protein powder
Pecan nuts
Almonds
Ground almonds
Pine nuts
Brazil nuts
Golden raisins
Dried cranberries
Dried dates
Dried currants

Cumin, ground
Coriander, ground
Sweet paprika
Sea salt
Mixed peppercorns
Cayenne pepper, ground
Caraway seeds
Chinese five-spice
Garam masala

In the refrigerator or freezer
Plain Greek-style yogurt
Fresh parmesan cheese
Cheddar cheese
Eggs
Blueberries, frozen
Raspberries, frozen
Gluten-free bread, frozen
Pizza bases/crusts, frozen
Rice milk
Fresh pasta

SOMETHING TO START THE DAY

Grabbing a bowl of cereal before rushing out the door is fine on a work day, but a leisurely breakfast on the weekend always feels so civilized.

Date and ginger muffins

1½ cups chopped dates
1 cup boiling water
⅓ cup golden syrup or honey
1 cup white rice flour
¾ cup soy flour
2 teaspoons baking powder
½ teaspoon baking soda
2 teaspoons ground ginger
½ teaspoon pumpkin pie spice
½ teaspoon xanthan gum
¼ teaspoon salt
2 tablespoons canola oil
1 egg
½ cup milk

1 Preheat the oven to 325°F. Grease a 12-cup standard muffin tin.

2 Combine the dates, boiling water, and golden syrup in a heatproof bowl and set aside to cool.

3 In another bowl, combine the rice flour, soy flour, baking powder, baking soda, ginger, pumpkin pie spice, xanthan gum, and salt.

4 In a separate bowl, whisk together the oil, egg, and milk, then add to the date mixture, stirring well. Pour into the dry ingredients and stir until all the ingredients are wet. Spoon the mixture into the muffin cups.

5 Bake for 20 minutes, or until nicely browned, turning the tin around after 10 minutes. Turn out to cool on a wire rack. Serve the muffins warm with butter.

Makes 12

Banana buttermilk pancakes

½ cup **Rice flour blend** (recipe page 9)
½ cup brown rice flour
2 tablespoons superfine sugar
1 teaspoon baking soda
1 teaspoon ground cinnamon
½ teaspoon salt
½ teaspoon vanilla extract
1 egg
about 1 cup buttermilk
1 overripe banana, mashed
pure maple syrup, to serve

1 In a bowl, mix together the Rice flour blend, brown rice flour, sugar, baking soda, cinnamon, and salt.

2 In a separate bowl, whisk together the vanilla, egg, and buttermilk, then add to the dry ingredients and whisk until there are no more lumps. Stir in the mashed banana and mix to distribute evenly. If the mixture seems a little thick, gradually add more buttermilk to achieve the desired consistency.

3 Heat a non-stick frying pan over medium heat and cook generous tablespoons of the batter until bubbles appear on the surface, then flip the pancake over and cook the other side.

4 Keep the cooked pancakes warm while you cook the remaining batter. Serve the pancakes with pure maple syrup.

Makes about 12 pancakes

Sweet potato loaf

This is a lovely, moist quick bread, which makes for a more filling breakfast than gluten-free toast.

1¾ cups **Rice flour blend** (recipe page 9)
2 teaspoons ground cinnamon
1 teaspoon baking powder
1 teaspoon baking soda
½ teaspoon xanthan gum
½ teaspoon salt
½ cup brown sugar
⅓ cup superfine sugar
⅓ cup canola oil
¼ cup buttermilk
3 eggs
7 oz sweet potato, grated
3 oz zucchini, grated
cinnamon sugar, to serve

1 Preheat the oven to 315°F. Grease a large bundt pan or ring mold.

2 In a bowl, combine the Rice flour blend, cinnamon, baking powder, baking soda, xanthan gum, and salt and stir to combine.

3 In a separate bowl, combine the brown sugar, superfine sugar, oil, buttermilk, and eggs and whisk well. Pour into the dry ingredients. Stir until smooth, then stir in the grated sweet potato and zucchini.

4 Spoon the batter into the prepared pan and bake for 1 hour or until cooked through and browned. Allow to firm up in the pan for 7–8 minutes, then turn out to cool on a wire rack, right side up.

5 Serve warm, spread with butter and sprinkled with cinnamon sugar.

Serves 8

Quinoa porridge

⅔ cup quinoa flakes
2 generous strips orange zest
½ teaspoon ground cinnamon
1 tablespoon currants
6 dried dates, pitted and chopped
salt, to taste
1 tablespoon chopped nuts
rice, soy, or dairy milk, to serve
pure maple syrup, to serve (optional)

1 In a small saucepan, bring 2 cups water to a boil, then add the quinoa, orange zest, cinnamon, currants, and dates. Reduce the heat to low and stir for about 2 minutes while it simmers and thickens.

2 Remove the saucepan from the heat and allow the porridge to cool a little, then remove the strips of zest and add a generous pinch of salt and the chopped nuts. Serve with milk and a drizzle of maple syrup if desired.

Serves 2–3

Protein bars

For this recipe use whichever combination of nuts, dried fruit, seeds, and juice you prefer, but keep the proportions the same.

½ cup protein powder

¼ cup quinoa flour

¼ cup **Rice flour blend** (recipe page 9)

2 teaspoons baking powder

½ teaspoon xanthan gum

½ teaspoon salt

⅓ cup cranberry juice

⅓ cup pure maple syrup

2 eggs

¼ cup pure nut butter

2 teaspoons canola oil

1 apple, grated

1 cup combined dried blueberries, cranberries, and dates, chopped to uniform size

1 cup combined unsalted pistachio nuts, almonds, and brazil nuts, roughly chopped

¼ cup shredded coconut

1 tablespoon sunflower seeds

1 Preheat the oven to 350°F. Line a 11 x 7-inch rectangular baking pan with a large piece of parchment paper, allowing the paper to overhang each end.

2 Put the protein powder, quinoa flour, Rice flour blend, baking powder, xanthan gum, and salt into a bowl and stir to combine.

3 In the bowl of a food processor, process the cranberry juice, maple syrup, eggs, nut butter, and oil until fully combined. Pour into the flour mixture and stir until there are no lumps, then add the grated apple, dried fruit, nuts, coconut, and sunflower seeds and stir until fully mixed.

4 Place the batter into the prepared pan, smooth the top, and bake for 20–25 minutes, or until evenly browned, turning the pan around after 10 minutes.

5 Remove the pan from the oven, carefully lift the slab out of the pan using the overhanging parchment paper, and slide off the paper onto a wire rack to cool. When cooled, cut into bars. Store in an airtight container for up to 3 days.

Makes about 20 pieces

Tip: *Nut butter is sold in the health food section of the supermarket and in health food stores.*

Bircher muesli with rosie-berry compote

In this recipe I use a sweeter Greek-style yogurt, which I buy in clear containers from the deli or health food store.

½ cup sweet plain Greek-style yogurt
½ cup milk
½ cup rolled rice flakes
1 heaping tablespoon ground nuts,
    such as macadamia nuts, pecans,
    or walnuts
salt, pinch or to taste
1 whole apple, unpeeled

Rosie-berry compote

1⅔ cups strawberries, rinsed,
    green tops removed, and diced
¼–½ teaspoon rosewater, to taste
sugar, pinch or to taste (optional)

1 Place the yogurt and milk into a bowl and whisk to combine. Stir in the rice flakes, nuts, and a pinch of salt, if desired, then cover the bowl and refrigerate overnight.

2 To make the rosie-berry compote, place half the diced strawberries into a small saucepan with 1 tablespoon water. Stir over low heat until the strawberries release their juice, then stir in the rosewater. Remove the pan from the heat and allow to cool a little, then stir in the remaining strawberries. Pour into a small glass bowl, cover, and refrigerate until required.

3 When ready to serve, grate the apple and stir it through the muesli. Place small portions into serving bowls and top with a little compote.

Serves 4–6

Tex-Mex breakfast

You can serve this as either a kick-starter breakfast or brunch.

Salsa
4 Roma (plum) tomatoes, quartered
1 red cayenne pepper, seeded and
    chopped
2 tablespoons chopped cilantro leaves
1 scallion, chopped
½ teaspoon salt, more to taste
cayenne pepper, pinch or to taste (optional)
freshly ground black pepper

¾ oz (1½ tablespoons) butter
4 eggs, lightly beaten
¼ cup grated cheddar cheese
4 corn tortillas

1 To make the salsa, put the tomatoes, pepper, cilantro, scallion, and salt into the bowl of a food processor and pulse until roughly chopped but not puréed. Add the cayenne pepper, if using, season with freshly ground black pepper and extra salt to taste, then drain the salsa in a colander set over a large bowl.

2 In a non-stick skillet over low heat, melt the butter and pour in the eggs. Gently stir the eggs, turning them over as they cook on the bottom, then add the cheese and continue stirring until the eggs are set to your liking. The longer they cook the more firm and dry the eggs will become.

3 Heat the tortillas according to the directions on the packet.

4 To serve, place one softened tortilla onto each serving plate and top with a quarter of the scrambled eggs. Top with some salsa and fold up to eat.

Serves 4

SOMETHING LIGHT

Whether it's snacks with drinks or a tasty light meal,
my family and friends all love my gluten-free treats.

Cheese and onion cornbread

Eat this cornbread hot from the oven, or slice and serve toasted, spread with garlic butter, and sprinkled with chili flakes.

¾ oz (1½ tablespoons) butter
1 tablespoon olive oil
3 large red onions, sliced
1 teaspoon crushed garlic
2 cups **Rice flour blend** (recipe page 9)
1 cup polenta
1 tablespoon mustard powder
1 tablespoon baking powder
1 teaspoon xanthan gum
2 teaspoons salt
1 cup grated gruyère or cheddar cheese
3 eggs
about 1¾ cups buttermilk

1 In a frying pan over low heat, melt the butter with the oil and fry the onions and garlic until very soft, about 15–20 minutes. Resist the temptation to eat the onions straight from the pan, and set aside to cool.

2 Preheat the oven to 350°F. Grease a 10-inch cast-iron skillet or frying pan with an ovenproof handle.

3 In a large bowl, combine the Rice flour blend, polenta, mustard powder, baking powder, xanthan gum, and salt. Whisk well to combine, then stir in the grated cheese.

4 In a small bowl, lightly whisk the eggs and buttermilk, then pour into the flour mixture. Add the cooled onions and stir until combined, adding a little more buttermilk if the mixture is too thick.

5 Spoon the mixture into the skillet and smooth the top. Bake for about 45 minutes, or until the cornbread is well browned and sounds hollow when tapped on the top. Remove the skillet from the oven and flip the cornbread out onto a wire rack to cool.

Makes one 10-inch round loaf

Zucchini fritters

2 cups grated zucchini
2 tablespoons olive oil
2 eggs
2 tablespoons white rice flour
2 tablespoons grated parmesan cheese
½ teaspoon salt
freshly ground black pepper, to taste
1 scallion, finely chopped
4 slices prosciutto or ham off the bone,
    finely chopped
2 teaspoons finely chopped basil
olive oil, for cooking
Tomato sauce, to serve
    (recipe page 48)
sour cream, to serve

1 Place the grated zucchini in a colander, squeeze out the excess moisture, and set aside to drain.

2 In a large bowl, whisk together the oil, eggs, rice flour, parmesan, salt, and freshly ground black pepper. Whisk until the batter is smooth, then stir in the zucchini, scallion, prosciutto, and basil and mix well.

3 Heat a little oil in a non-stick frying pan over medium heat and cook tablespoons of the zucchini mixture on both sides until browned and set.

4 Serve warm with the Tomato sauce and a dollop of sour cream.

Makes 8–10 fritters; serves 4 as part of a light meal

Chili coconut crab cakes

For this recipe I use a good quality, commercially prepared crabmeat, which you'll find in plastic tubs in the refrigerator section of the supermarket or fish market. Don't be concerned if the chili jam tastes a bit too fiery at first, as it mellows very nicely overnight. It will also thicken up once it's refrigerated, so if you prefer a liquid sauce rather than a jam consistency, simply thin with a little water.

Sweet chili jam

5 long red chilies, seeds and
    membranes removed
½ red onion, layers separated
1 large garlic clove, peeled and halved
½ cup brown sugar
¼ cup rice vinegar
1 tablespoon fish sauce
1 teaspoon grated fresh ginger

Crab cakes

2 cups coconut milk, well shaken
1 cup arborio rice
salt, to taste
2 eggs, lightly beaten
1 kaffir lime leaf, finely chopped
1 tablespoon cilantro leaves, finely
    chopped
2 teaspoons lime juice
2 teaspoons fish sauce
½–1 teaspoon crushed red chili flakes,
    to taste
4 oz prepared crabmeat
oil, for cooking

1 Preheat the oven to 350°F. To make the sweet chili jam, roughly chop the chilies and put them in a roasting pan with the onion and garlic and roast for 20–30 minutes, or until softened. Set aside to cool, then transfer to the bowl of a food processor along with ¼ cup water. Purée, stopping to scrape down the side of the bowl a few times.

2 Place the purée into a saucepan with the brown sugar, vinegar, fish sauce, and ginger. Cover and simmer over low heat until thickened, about 20 minutes. Remove the pan from the heat and pour the chili jam into a glass container, then cover and refrigerate for at least 24 hours and up to 1 week.

3 To make the crab cakes, put the coconut milk, rice, and a generous pinch of salt in a saucepan with a lid. Bring to a boil over high heat, then reduce the heat to low, cover, and simmer for 10 minutes. Remove the pan from the heat and stir the rice, then cover and set aside until the rice is cool enough to handle.

4 In a glass or stainless-steel bowl, combine the eggs, lime leaf, cilantro, lime juice, fish sauce, and crushed chili flakes and stir until well combined. Add the coconut rice to the bowl and mix well, then add the crabmeat and stir until fully incorporated. Using wet hands, firmly squeeze the mixture into small, flattened cakes.

5 Heat a little oil in a non-stick frying pan and cook the crab cakes over medium heat until browned on each side and the egg has set. Cover the pan with a lid to help the egg to set. Serve warm with a little of the sweet chili jam on top.

Makes about 40 bite-sized crab cakes

Roast pepper and walnut dip

This dip is best prepared ahead to allow the flavors to develop, and by all means add some chili or harissa paste to spice it up.

3 large red bell peppers
½ cup walnuts
1 tablespoon tomato paste
    (concentrated purée)
1 tablespoon olive oil
2 teaspoons brown sugar
1 teaspoon balsamic vinegar

1 Cut the peppers into quarters, then remove the seeds and membranes and grill (or broil) on both sides until the skin is blackened and the flesh softened. While the peppers are still hot, put into a small bowl, cover with plastic wrap, and set aside until cool enough to handle.

2 Pull off the pepper skins and discard, then place the peppers into the bowl of a food processor with the rest of the ingredients and process until the pepper is smooth and the nuts are chopped into fairly small pieces.

3 Serve with crackers or vegetable sticks, or use as a condiment for barbecued steak or lamb.

Makes 1 cup

Tip: *You will need about 10 oz prepared peppers (once stems, seeds and membranes are removed).*

Baba ghanoush

Serve baba ghanoush as a dip, spread, or as an accompaniment to meat dishes.

1 tablespoon olive oil
2 eggplants, generous 1 lb in total
1 tablespoon tahini
1 tablespoon lemon juice
½ teaspoon crushed garlic
¼ teaspoon ground cumin
¼ teaspoon sweet paprika
½ teaspoon salt
black pepper, to taste
2 tablespoons total combined chopped
    herbs, such as parsley, mint, and
    cilantro leaves

1 Preheat the oven to 350°F.

2 Rub the oil over the eggplants and poke several holes in the skin with a skewer so they don't explode when cooked. Place onto a baking sheet and bake for about 45 minutes, or until very wrinkled and soft. Set aside until cool, then cut in half, scoop out the flesh, and discard the skin.

3 Put the eggplant into the bowl of a food processor along with the tahini, lemon juice, garlic, cumin, paprika, salt, and a good grind of black pepper. Process to the desired consistency.

4 Stir in the herbs and season to taste with extra salt and pepper, then spoon into a bowl, cover, and refrigerate overnight. Check the seasoning again before serving at room temperature.

Makes about 2 cups

Sausage rolls

For this recipe I usually buy gluten-free sausages from the butcher, as it's one less job I have to do, but by all means make up your favor-ite meat filling if you prefer.

1 quantity **Potato pastry** (recipe
    page 170)
1 lb gluten-free sausages
Tomato sauce, to serve (optional)
    (recipe page 48)

1 Preheat the oven to 350°F and line two baking sheets with parchment paper.

2 Roll out one round of Potato pastry between two sheets of parchment paper into a roughly rectangular shape, then turn the pastry over to smooth out any creases on the back. Remove the top sheet of parchment paper and, starting about 1¼ inches inside the long edge of the pastry, squeeze the sausage meat out of the casing, parallel to the edge of the pastry. Using the parchment paper to lift, roll the pastry over to cover the sausage meat and then cut off the excess pastry. Press gently on the seam to seal, then patch any holes and lightly roll back and forth with your hands to smooth the pastry. Repeat with the second round of pastry.

3 Cut the long sausage rolls into 2-inch lengths, or as preferred, place onto the prepared baking sheets, and bake for about 35 minutes, or until evenly browned, turning the baking sheets around twice. Serve with Tomato sauce if desired.

Makes 15–18 sausage rolls

Spinach and ricotta pies

It's fine to use frozen spinach instead of fresh in this recipe, but make sure you buy fresh ricotta from the deli and not the ricotta in tubs, as the fresh cheese makes a huge difference to the flavor.

1 tablespoon olive oil

1 leek, white part only, washed well and sliced

½ teaspoon crushed garlic

1 lb spinach, trimmed and washed

¼ teaspoon grated fresh nutmeg

salt and pepper, to taste

3 large eggs

1 lb fresh ricotta cheese

½ cup grated parmesan cheese

¼ cup crumbled plain feta cheese

¼ cup grated mozzarella cheese

1 handful basil leaves, chopped

2 tablespoons pine nuts, toasted and chopped

1 Preheat the oven to 325°F. Grease a 12-cup standard muffin tin.

2 Heat the oil in a large frying pan and cook the leek and garlic for 5 minutes, or until softened, then add the spinach and cook for a few more minutes until wilted. Pour off any excess liquid and season with the nutmeg and salt and pepper to taste.

3 Put the eggs, ricotta, parmesan, feta, and mozzarella cheeses into the bowl of a food processor and process until smooth, stopping a few times to scrape down the side of the bowl. Pour into a large mixing bowl, add the spinach mixture, basil, and pine nuts and stir until fully combined. This step may seem like it's just making extra washing up, but if you add the spinach and basil in the food processor the mixture gets too puréed and you'll end up with completely green food.

4 Pour the mixture into the prepared muffin tin, filling each hole generously, and bake for about 25 minutes, or until set and lightly browned on top. Serve warm or at room temperature.

Makes 12

Sushi

I know homemade sushi might seem a bit too fiddly to bother with, but you quickly get the hang of it and by making your own you can try all sorts of fillings that might otherwise be too risky to eat at a restaurant.

1 cup sushi rice
2 tablespoons rice vinegar
1 tablespoon dry sherry (optional)
2 teaspoons superfine sugar
½ teaspoon salt
4–6 nori sheets
soy sauce, to serve

Toppings and fillings
mayonnaise
avocado, mashed with lime juice
wasabi paste
sour cream with chopped chives
cream cheese
smoked salmon, chopped
Teriyaki picnic pork, shredded
 (recipe page 85)
grilled shrimp, chopped
scallions, chopped
chives, snipped
crabmeat
tuna in oil, drained
fish roe
red onion, finely diced
roasted bell pepper, sliced
cucumber, cut into strips
carrot, grated
lettuce, shredded
sprouts
hard-boiled egg, chopped

1 Place the rice and 1½ cups water into a saucepan and bring to a boil, then reduce the heat to low and simmer for 12 minutes. Turn off the heat and leave the rice to stand, covered with the lid, for another 15 minutes.

2 Meanwhile, combine the vinegar, sherry, sugar, and salt in a small saucepan and simmer, stirring until the sugar melts. Allow to cool.

3 Put the cooked rice into an open shallow baking dish and pour over the vinegar mixture. Stir gently to combine, then cover with a clean dish towel and leave to cool.

4 Place one nori sheet, shiny side down and with the long edge nearest to you, onto a sushi mat. Using wet fingers, place some of the rice along the ¾ inch inside the closest edge, then lay your choice of filling on top. Cover with more rice to enclose the filling, then using the mat, roll the nori sheet firmly around the filling. Moisten along the edge to seal, then roll tightly in plastic wrap and refrigerate until needed.

5 To serve, discard the plastic wrap and slice the sushi to the required size using a very sharp knife. Wipe the blade after each cut to prevent the rice sticking. Serve the sushi cold with small bowls of soy sauce for dipping.

Makes 4–6 full-size rolls

Tip: *For sushi canapés, make the rolls as above but without the filling. Cut the rolls into smaller bite-sized slices and place the filling on the top.*

Chicken noodle soup

One for the children

2 cups **Chicken broth** (recipe page 168)

2 teaspoons cornstarch

1 teaspoon chicken bouillon

1 handful dried rice noodles

¼ teaspoon dried tarragon

about ½ cup chopped cooked chicken

1 In a saucepan, heat the broth until boiling. In a small bowl, make a slurry with the cornstarch, bouillon, and 2 tablespoons of hot broth, then return to the saucepan and stir until slightly thickened.

2 Break the rice noodles into smaller pieces and add to the soup along with the tarragon and chicken. Simmer until the noodles have softened and the chicken has heated through.

Serves 2 children

One for the adults

4 cups **Chicken broth** (recipe page 168)

¼–½ teaspoon green curry paste, to taste

1 tablespoon fish sauce

1 tablespoon lime juice

1 small baby bok choy, shredded

1 handful dried rice noodles

about 1 cup chopped cooked chicken

1 tablespoon chopped cilantro leaves

1 handful bean sprouts

1 In a large saucepan, heat the broth until boiling, then add the curry paste, fish sauce, lime juice, bok choy, rice noodles, and chopped chicken.

2 Simmer until the noodles have softened and the chicken has heated through. Stir in the cilantro and bean sprouts and serve.

Serves 2 adults

Eggplant rolls

White bean and pesto purée

14 oz can white beans, rinsed and
    drained
2 tablespoons fresh ricotta cheese
1 tablespoon pesto
2 teaspoons lemon juice

Tomato sauce

1 onion, finely diced
1 tablespoon olive oil
1 teaspoon crushed garlic
½ cup white wine
24 fl oz bottle tomato passata
    (puréed tomatoes)
1 bay leaf
pinch sugar

1 large eggplant
olive oil

1 To make the white bean and pesto purée, place the beans, ricotta, pesto, and lemon juice into the bowl of a food processor and blend until well combined, stopping to scrape down the side of the bowl a few times. Set aside.

2 To make the Tomato sauce, cook the onion in the oil in a saucepan over low heat until very soft. Add the garlic, white wine, tomato passata, bay leaf, and sugar and simmer until the sauce is thickened, stirring occasionally. Set aside.

3 Preheat the oven to 350°F.

4 Cut the eggplant lengthways into ½-inch slices, then brush each slice with a little olive oil and grill (or broil) on both sides until cooked through. When cool enough to handle, spread a tablespoon of the white bean purée over each slice and roll up the eggplant, beginning at the narrow end. Place the rolls, seam side down, into an ovenproof dish. Cover the dish with foil and warm in the oven.

5 To serve, ladle a puddle of Tomato sauce onto a serving plate, then place one or two eggplant rolls in the middle and top with a little extra white bean purée if desired.

Makes 6–8 eggplant rolls

Tips: *The white bean and pesto purée also makes a tasty dip. Any leftover tomato sauce is suitable to freeze, or can be served with* **Sausage rolls** *(recipe page 40) or* **Zucchini fritters** *(recipe page 32).*

Spinach and lemon pilaf

1 cup wild blend rice
1 tablespoon olive oil
1 teaspoon crushed garlic
1 bunch spinach, washed and trimmed
1 teaspoon salt
black pepper, to taste
¼ cup lemon juice
3 scallions, chopped
1 large handful flat-leaf (Italian) parsley,
    chopped
1 tablespoon chopped dill
1 tablespoon capers, rinsed

1 Place the rice and 1½ cups water into a saucepan, cover, and bring to a boil. Reduce the heat to low and simmer until all of the water is absorbed, then fluff the rice with a fork and set aside, covered, for another 10 minutes.

2 In a frying pan, heat the oil and garlic, then add the spinach and stir until the spinach is tender and is wilted a little. Drain off the excess liquid, remove the spinach from the pan and chop. Stir the spinach into the rice along with salt, a good grind of black pepper, and the lemon juice.

3 When ready to serve, stir in the scallions, parsley, dill, and capers and season to taste with extra salt and freshly ground black pepper. Serve with **Baked salmon with dill** (recipe page 109) or **Grilled haloumi salad** (recipe page 60).

Serves 6 as a side dish

Falafel slice

14 oz can chickpeas, rinsed and drained
1 cup fresh ricotta cheese
3 eggs, separated
2 oz plain feta cheese
1 scallion, roughly chopped
1 tablespoon lemon juice
1 tablespoon tahini
1 teaspoon crushed garlic
¾ teaspoon ground cumin
¾ teaspoon ground coriander
½ teaspoon salt
black pepper, to taste
¼ cup combined chopped herbs,
    including parsley, mint, and
    cilantro leaves
1 small zucchini (3-4 oz), grated
    and drained

1 Preheat the oven to 350°F. Grease a 9- or 10-inch round springform pan and line the base of the pan with parchment paper.

2 In the bowl of a food processor, combine the chickpeas, ricotta, egg yolks, feta, scallion, lemon juice, tahini, garlic, cumin, coriander, salt, and a good grind of black pepper. Process to a fairly smooth paste. Place into a large mixing bowl and stir in the chopped herbs and grated zucchini.

3 In a separate bowl and using electric beaters, beat the egg whites to stiff peak stage, then gently fold into the ricotta mixture.

4 Pour into the prepared pan and bake for about 45 minutes, or until nicely browned on top. Serve warm or at room temperature with **Beet salad** (recipe page 68).

Serves 8

Ham and Swiss quiche

If you prefer larger pieces of ham in your quiche, chop the ham separately and scatter over the base before pouring in the egg mixture.

½ quantity **Potato pastry** (recipe page 170)
⅓ cup grated Swiss or Jarlsberg cheese
3 eggs
½ cup mascarpone cheese
½ cup milk
3 oz ham off the bone, chopped
1 teaspoon French mustard

1 Preheat the oven to 325°F. Lightly grease the base of a 9½-inch loose-based quiche/tart pan.

2 Roll out the pastry between two sheets of parchment paper into a circle large enough to fit the pan, smoothing any creases on the back. Remove the top sheet of parchment paper, then flip the pastry over and gently press into the base and side of the pan, removing the second sheet of parchment paper as you go. Trim the excess pastry around the top, patch any holes with pastry scraps, and prick the base a few times with a skewer.

3 Place one of the sheets of parchment paper into the pan, fill with pie weights or dried beans, and blind bake the pastry for 10 minutes. Remove the parchment paper and pie weights and bake the pastry for another 10 minutes, or until dry. Remove the pan from the oven and use a little of the grated cheese to patch any obvious holes so the filling doesn't run through and stick to the pan. Reduce the oven temperature to 315°F.

4 In the bowl of a food processor, process the eggs, mascarpone, milk, ham, mustard, and remaining cheese until smooth.

5 Put the pan onto a baking sheet and pour in the egg mixture, then bake for about 20 minutes, or until set and the top is evenly browned. The filling will puff up a little during baking but settles back on cooling. Allow the quiche to firm up in the pan for a few minutes before serving with a green salad.

Serves 6

Chicken salad with creamy tarragon dressing

This delicious salad works just as well if you substitute cold poached salmon for the chicken.

3 single boneless, skinless chicken
    breasts
1 lb baby potatoes, unpeeled
8 oz green beans
1 tablespoon diced red onion
salt and freshly ground black pepper,
    to taste
Romaine lettuce or arugula, chopped,
    to serve

Dressing
2 hard-boiled eggs, shelled
2 tablespoons white wine vinegar
1 tablespoon Dijon mustard
½ cup olive oil
2 tablespoons finely chopped tarragon

1 Put the chicken breasts in a saucepan with water to cover, bring to a boil, then immediately reduce the heat to a very gentle simmer and poach for 5–7 minutes, depending on the thickness of the chicken. Put into a bowl with enough of the poaching liquid to cover and refrigerate until cooled.

2 Steam the potatoes until soft, then cover and refrigerate until needed. Top and tail the beans and briefly blanch in boiling water, then place into a bowl of ice water to stop the cooking process. Refrigerate until needed.

3 To make the dressing, put the boiled eggs, vinegar, and mustard into the bowl of a food processor. Process to a smooth paste, scraping down the side of the bowl. Then, with the motor running, slowly add the olive oil. Add the tarragon and pulse briefly. Pour the dressing into a bowl, cover with plastic wrap and refrigerate for at least 3 hours.

4 To assemble the salad, slice the drained chicken into bite-sized pieces. Chop the steamed potatoes and blanched beans into smaller pieces if necessary.

5 Put the chicken, potatoes, beans, and onion into a large bowl and pour over the dressing. Toss gently to mix, season with salt and freshly ground black pepper to taste, then serve on a bed of chopped lettuce or arugula.

Serves 4 as a main course salad

Tip: *It's a good idea to steam the potatoes rather than boil them, as boiling can make the potatoes too wet.*

Brown rice salad with chili vinaigrette

This is good for a portable lunch because it can be prepared ahead, doesn't require heating, and is very filling. Try to find center-cut bacon, as this has more meat and less fat than other cuts.

Chili vinaigrette

1 long red cayenne chili
¼ cup olive oil
2 tablespoons lemon juice
1 teaspoon Dijon mustard
¼ teaspoon crushed garlic
¼ teaspoon cayenne pepper
salt and freshly ground black pepper,
    to taste

Rice salad

4 cups cooked brown rice
14 oz can artichokes, drained and
    rinsed, chopped
¼ small red onion, finely diced
4 oz center-cut bacon, diced, cooked,
    and drained
7 oz cucumber, seeded and diced
2 tablespoons chopped flat-leaf
    (Italian) parsley
1 tablespoon chopped mint

1 To make the Chili vinaigrette, cut a long slit in the chili and open out. Discard the seeds and membranes and finely dice the chili. In a jar with a lid, combine all the vinaigrette ingredients, season with salt and pepper, and shake vigorously until well combined. Set aside for at least 30 minutes for the flavors to develop.

2 Meanwhile, to make the Rice salad, combine all the ingredients in a large bowl and mix well. Pour the vinaigrette over the salad and mix until evenly coated.

Serves 6 as a side salad; 3–4 as a main course salad

Grilled haloumi salad with caper dressing

Caper dressing

2 tablespoons olive oil
1 tablespoon lemon juice
1 tablespoon white wine vinegar
1 tablespoon capers
1 teaspoon crushed garlic
1 teaspoon Dijon mustard
pinch dried oregano
salt and pepper, to taste

Haloumi salad

8 oz haloumi cheese
3 zucchini
14 oz can artichokes, drained
1 lemon
2 tablespoons olive oil

1 To make the Caper dressing, combine all ingredients in a glass jar with a lid. Season with salt and pepper and shake vigorously to combine. Allow the dressing to stand for 30 minutes for the flavors to develop.

2 To make the haloumi salad, cut the haloumi into eight slices. Halve the zucchini lengthways and chop each half into three chunks. Halve the artichokes.

3 Cut the lemon into quarters and place into a bowl along with the haloumi, zucchini, artichokes, and olive oil. Toss gently to coat with the oil.

4 Place all the pieces onto a flat grill plate and cook until well browned on all sides. Pile onto a warmed serving dish and drizzle the caper dressing over the warm vegetables.

Serves 4 as a side salad

Tomato, corn and black bean salad

Be careful not to confuse canned black beans with the fermented black beans used in Asian recipes. I buy dried black beans from the health food store, cook up a big batch in the pressure cooker, and freeze what I don't use. If that all sounds a bit too hard, substitute whichever beans you prefer, but the color contrast won't be as striking.

1 cup cooked corn kernels
1 cup cooked (or canned) black beans
1 cup seeded and diced Roma (plum) tomatoes
1 tablespoon finely diced red onion
¼ cup olive oil
1 tablespoon lime juice
¼ teaspoon ground cumin
cayenne pepper, to taste (optional)
salt and pepper, to taste

1 In a large bowl, combine the corn, beans, tomato, and onion and toss to mix.

2 In a glass jar with a lid, combine the olive oil, lime juice, cumin, and cayenne pepper, if using. Season to taste with salt and pepper. Shake the jar vigorously to combine. Pour the dressing over the salad and set aside for 30 minutes for the flavors to develop. Serve at room temperature.

Serves 4 as a side salad

Asian-style coleslaw

2 large carrots, grated

¼ yellow bell pepper, seeded and
thinly sliced

2 cups shredded green cabbage

2 cups shredded red cabbage

3 scallions, thinly sliced

¼ cup finely chopped combined mint,
Vietnamese mint, and cilantro leaves

1 long red chili, seeded and finely
chopped

1 teaspoon sesame seeds

2 tablespoons peanut oil

1 tablespoon lime juice

2 teaspoons fish sauce

1 teaspoon superfine sugar

1 handful bean sprouts, rinsed

1 In a large bowl, combine the carrot, bell pepper, cabbage, scallions, herbs, chili, and sesame seeds and toss to combine.

2 In a glass jar with a lid, combine the peanut oil, lime juice, fish sauce, and sugar and shake vigorously until the sugar has dissolved. Pour the dressing over the salad and toss to coat.

3 Cover the bowl and set the salad aside for 1 hour or so for the flavors to mellow. Just before serving, add the bean sprouts and toss again to combine.

Serves 6 as a side salad

Tip: *If you plan to use Chinese cabbage in this salad, add it just before serving as it wilts very quickly.*

Caraway-spiced red cabbage

This is such a versatile recipe that is not only healthy and quick to make, but its rich red color always looks so striking on the plate. It complements most pork dishes.

2 leeks, white part only, washed and
    sliced
1 tablespoon olive oil
1 lb red cabbage, outer leaves and
    center stalk discarded, shredded
1 green cooking apple, unpeeled, grated
1½ teaspoons caraway seeds

1 In a large saucepan over medium heat, sauté the leeks in the olive oil for a few minutes until soft.

2 Add the cabbage along with the grated apple and caraway seeds. Stir until well combined, then reduce the heat to low, cover the pan, and cook for 5 minutes, or until the cabbage has softened a little. Serve warm.

Serves 6 as a side dish

Beet salad

4 beets, washed
¼ cup orange juice
2 tablespoons olive oil
2 tablespoons currants
1 tablespoon white wine vinegar
salt and freshly ground black pepper,
    to taste
½ red onion, finely diced
2 cups arugula
½ cup crumbled plain feta cheese
2 tablespoons pine nuts, toasted

1 Preheat the oven to 350°F. Wrap the beets individually in foil and bake for 1 hour, or until a skewer pushes through easily (the cooking time will vary depending on the size of the beet). Alternatively, steam the beets in a pressure cooker according to the manufacturer's instructions. When cool enough to handle, rub off the skins and cut the beets into wedges.

2 Whisk together the orange juice, olive oil, currants, and vinegar and season with salt and pepper.

3 In a bowl, combine the beet wedges and onion, then pour over the dressing and toss gently to coat.

4 Spread the arugula onto a serving plate and top with the beet salad, then just before serving sprinkle with the feta cheese and pine nuts.

Serves 4–6 as a side salad

SOMETHING MORE SUBSTANTIAL

Sharing food and wine with good friends is one of life's great pleasures, and certainly not one that I'm going to miss out on because of a restricted diet.

Sweet potato dahl

1 red onion, diced
1 teaspoon crushed garlic
1 teaspoon grated fresh ginger
1 tablespoon mustard seed oil or
    canola oil
1 tablespoon Madras curry paste
1 cup split red lentils, rinsed
8 oz grated sweet potato
½ teaspoon garam masala
salt, to taste

Mint and cucumber raita
1 cup plain Greek-style yogurt
1 short cucumber, seeded and cut
    into small dice
¼ small red onion, finely diced
3 tablespoons finely chopped mint
¼ teaspoon ground cumin
¼ teaspoon salt
pinch sugar
pinch cayenne pepper

1 In a heavy-based saucepan over medium heat, sauté the onion, garlic, and ginger in the oil for 5 minutes, or until the onion is soft.

2 Add the curry paste and cook until fragrant, then increase the heat and add the lentils and sweet potato. Stir over high heat for 1–2 minutes to toast the lentils slightly, then reduce the heat to low, add 2 cups water, and stir well to loosen the brown residue on the bottom of the pan. Cover and simmer for about 15 minutes, or until the lentils have softened.

3 Add the garam masala, stir again to combine, then cover the pan and set aside for 10 minutes.

4 Meanwhile, make the Mint and cucumber raita. Combine the yogurt with the remaining ingredients in a bowl and mix well. Set aside.

5 Season the dahl with salt, to taste. Serve warm as a side dish, or as a main dish with papadums, rice, and the raita.

Serves 6 as a side dish; 4 as a main dish

Green pea risotto in the pressure cooker

I love the idea of dinner parties with glamorous friends swapping amusing stories while I leisurely spoon hot broth over expensive rice, but the reality in my house is a cranky six-year-old demanding food NOW. I consider my pressure cooker indispensable in the kitchen, but risotto purists might like to turn the page.

1 tablespoon olive oil
1½ oz (3 tablespoons) butter
2 leeks, white part only, washed and
    sliced
1 generous teaspoon crushed garlic
1½ cups arborio rice
½ cup white wine
2 cups **Chicken broth** (recipe page 168)
1 cup shelled peas
¼ cup freshly grated parmesan cheese
1 tablespoon chopped basil
½ teaspoon salt, plus more to taste
freshly ground black pepper, to taste
grated parmesan cheese, extra, to serve

1 In a pressure cooker, heat the olive oil and half of the butter and sauté the leeks and garlic until softened, then add the rice and stir to coat. Add the wine and when it has almost absorbed, stir in the broth and 1½ cups water. Lock the lid in place and bring to full pressure, then reduce the temperature and cook for 6 minutes.

2 Cook the peas in salted boiling water, then drain and keep warm.

3 Remove the cooker from the heat and quick-release the pressure, according to the manufacturer's instructions. Stir in the remaining butter and the peas, parmesan, basil, and ½ teaspoon salt. Replace the lid and set aside for 1–2 minutes.

4 To serve, season to taste with extra salt and pepper and offer extra grated parmesan cheese separately.

Serves 4

Steamed porkupines

1½ cups glutinous white rice
8 oz can water chestnuts, drained
1 scallion, including the green stem,
    roughly chopped
1 tablespoon soy sauce
1 tablespoon oyster sauce
1 teaspoon grated fresh ginger
1 teaspoon crushed garlic
1 teaspoon fish sauce
1 lb minced (ground) pork

1 Rinse the rice in a sieve, then put into a bowl, cover with water, and leave to stand overnight.

2 Place the water chestnuts, scallion, soy sauce, oyster sauce, ginger, garlic, and fish sauce into the bowl of a food processor and process until the water chestnuts are finely minced, stopping to scrape down the side of the bowl a couple of times. Add the pork and process briefly to make a fairly smooth paste.

3 Drain the rice and place in a pile on a plate. Using wet hands, roll teaspoons of the pork mixture into balls and then roll in the rice, pressing firmly to adhere.

4 Add 2–3 cups water to a large saucepan or wok with a lid, bring to a boil, then reduce the heat to a gentle simmer. Line a flat-bottomed metal or bamboo steamer with parchment paper and poke a few small holes in the paper to allow excess moisture to drip through. Place six or seven porkupines into the steamer basket, leaving space around each one so they don't touch and stick together while they cook. Cover the pan with the lid and steam for 25 minutes, or until the rice is translucent and cooked through. Repeat with the remaining mixture, adding boiling water to the pan as needed.

5 Serve with **Sweet and sour stir-fried vegetables** (recipe page 78) as a main course, or as an appetizer with a little **Sweet chili jam** (recipe page 35).

Makes about 30

Sweet and sour stir-fried vegetables

1 tablespoon vegetable oil

½ red bell pepper, seeded and
    thinly sliced

1 red onion, cut into thin wedges

1 teaspoon crushed garlic

1 teaspoon crushed fresh ginger

6 baby corn, quartered lengthways

1 zucchini, cut into thin strips

1 carrot, cut into thin strips

¾ cup **Sweet and sour sauce**
    (recipe page 168)

1 cup finely shredded red cabbage

2 scallions, cut into thin strips

1 handful bean sprouts, rinsed

cooked brown rice, to serve

1 Heat the oil in a wok over high heat, swirling to coat the base and side, then add the bell pepper, onion, garlic, and ginger. Keep the ingredients moving around the wok for 4–5 minutes, or until the onion has softened, then add the corn, zucchini, and carrot and continue cooking for a few minutes.

2 Reduce the heat a little and pour in the Sweet and sour sauce, stir to coat the vegetables, then cover the wok and simmer for a few minutes. Just before serving, add the cabbage, scallions, and bean sprouts and stir again to combine and heat through. Serve immediately with brown rice.

Serves 4 as part of a main course

Herbed lentil pilaf

2 tablespoons olive oil
1 red onion, diced
1 tablespoon ground coriander
2 teaspoons crushed garlic
1 cup basmati rice
14 oz can lentils, rinsed and drained
3 scallions, finely chopped
1 large handful flat-leaf (Italian) parsley,
   chopped
1 large handful cilantro leaves, chopped
1 handful mint, chopped

Dressing
⅓ cup olive oil
2 tablespoons currants
2 tablespoons lemon juice
2 teaspoons white wine vinegar
pinch sweet paprika
½ teaspoon salt
freshly ground black pepper, to taste

1 In a large saucepan, heat the oil and cook the onion, ground coriander, and garlic over low heat for 5 minutes, or until the onion has softened. Stir in the rice and 2 cups water, cover the pan, and bring to a boil. Reduce the heat and simmer gently for about 10 minutes, or until all the liquid is absorbed. Remove the pan from the heat, fluff the rice with a fork, and leave covered for another 10 minutes.

2 Meanwhile, make the dressing. In a glass jar with a lid, combine the oil, currants, lemon juice, vinegar, paprika, salt, and a generous grind of black pepper. Shake vigorously to mix.

3 Add the lentils to the warm rice along with the scallions and herbs, then pour over the dressing and mix well. Serve the warm pilaf with **Moroccan ground lamb** (recipe page 82) or **Braised lamb shanks** (recipe page 114).

Serves 6 as a side dish

Moroccan ground lamb with feta and yogurt sauce

2 tablespoons olive oil
1 red onion, diced
1 teaspoon ground coriander
1 teaspoon ground cumin
2 teaspoons crushed garlic
1 lb minced (ground) lamb
½ teaspoon ground cinnamon
½ teaspoon allspice
2 tablespoons tomato paste
   (concentrated purée)
¼ cup pine nuts, toasted
½ teaspoon salt
¼ teaspoon freshly ground black pepper
¼ teaspoon cayenne pepper (optional)
1 handful mint, chopped

Feta and yogurt sauce
3-4 oz plain feta cheese
2 tablespoons plain Greek-style yogurt
2 teaspoons lemon juice

1 In a frying pan with a lid, heat the oil and cook the onion, coriander, cumin, and garlic for about 5 minutes, or until the onion is soft.

2 Increase the heat to high and add the lamb, browning quickly and breaking up any lumps as you go. Stir in the cinnamon, allspice, tomato paste, toasted pine nuts, and ½ cup water. Reduce the heat to low, cover the pan, and simmer for a few minutes until the liquid has absorbed. Season with salt, pepper, and cayenne pepper, if using.

3 To make the feta and yogurt sauce, put the feta cheese, yogurt, lemon juice, and 3–4 tablespoons water in a food processor. Blend to make a smooth sauce, stopping to scrape down the side of the bowl a few times.

4 Serve the lamb warm, drizzled with the sauce and sprinkled with chopped mint, with **Herbed lentil pilaf** (recipe page 81) and **Baba ghanoush** (recipe page 39) on the side.

Serves 4 as part of a main meal

Teriyaki picnic pork

I usually make this to serve cold the following day with coleslaw, but it's also perfect as a hot main course dish.

Marinade
¼ cup soy sauce
2 tablespoons rice vinegar
1 tablespoon vegetable oil
1 tablespoon honey
1 tablespoon sherry
1 teaspoon crushed garlic
1 teaspoon grated ginger

1 lb 8 oz pork tenderloin fillets

1 In a large bowl, mix all the marinade ingredients together, then add the pork fillets, turning a few times to coat with the marinade. Cover the bowl and refrigerate overnight.

2 Preheat the oven to 350°F and lightly grease a roasting pan.

3 Place the pork in the pan, tucking under the thin end to make a fairly even thickness. Bake the pork for 20–25 minutes, depending on the thickness of the fillet, turning it over twice and brushing with the cooking juices to create an even glaze.

4 Pour the marinade into a small saucepan, bring to a boil, and simmer for 5 minutes, or until slightly reduced. Pour into a clean bowl to use as a dipping sauce.

5 When the pork is cooked, wrap in double foil and set aside to rest for 10 minutes before serving, or refrigerate overnight for picnic pork and serve with **Asian-style coleslaw** (recipe page 64).

Serves 6 as part of a main meal

Vitello tonnato

Excellent for a summer lunch or picnic, Vitello tonnato is best prepared a day ahead and then assembled just before serving.

Tuna mayonnaise

2 egg yolks
1 teaspoon Dijon mustard
1 cup grapeseed oil
3-5 oz canned tuna in oil, drained
1 tablespoon capers, rinsed
3 anchovies, rinsed
2 tablespoons lemon juice
salt and pepper, to taste

Poached veal

1 lb 8 oz boneless veal roast, leg or loin
1 cup white wine
1 onion, quartered
1 carrot, chopped
1 celery stalk, chopped
1 rosemary sprig
1 bay leaf
¼ lemon
few peppercorns
1 tablespoon capers, rinsed

1 To make the Tuna mayonnaise, put the egg yolks and mustard in a food processor and blend to combine. With the motor running, very gradually add the oil. Add the tuna, capers, anchovies, and lemon juice and blend until well combined and thickened. Season to taste with salt and pepper, then cover and refrigerate overnight. Whisk well and check the seasoning again before serving.

2 To make the poached veal, place all the ingredients, except the capers, into a large saucepan with a lid and add enough water to cover. Cover with the lid, bring to a boil, then reduce the heat and simmer very gently for 1½–2 hours, or until the veal is fork-tender, skimming the surface as necessary. Remove the pan from the stove and allow the veal to cool completely in its cooking liquid in the refrigerator.

3 When fully cooled, remove the veal from the broth, wrap tightly in foil, and refrigerate until needed. Strain the broth and freeze in batches for another use.

4 About 30 minutes before serving, cut the veal into thin slices and arrange in a single layer on a serving plate. Set aside, loosely covered, to bring to room temperature. Just before serving, drizzle over the tuna mayonnaise and sprinkle with capers.

Serves 4–6

Tip: *If your refrigerator is large enough, you can leave the veal in the saucepan to cool. Alternatively, transfer it to a glass bowl with enough of the poaching liquid to cover and store, covered with plastic wrap, in the refrigerator.*

Pad Thai

¼ cup boiling water

2 teaspoons pure tamarind pulp

2 tablespoons brown sugar

2 tablespoons fish sauce

2 tablespoons peanut oil

1 tablespoon tomato paste
   (concentrated purée)

1 tablespoon soy sauce

1 teaspoon crushed chili flakes

8 oz dried rice noodles

2 teaspoons peanut oil, extra

1 egg, lightly beaten

2 teaspoons crushed garlic

2 teaspoons grated fresh ginger

1 red onion, cut into thin wedges

1 lb minced (ground) chicken

2 cups chopped Chinese cabbage

1 cup sliced snow peas

1 cup sliced scallions

1 cup bean sprouts, rinsed

1 tablespoon finely chopped cilantro
   leaves

1 tablespoon lime juice

1 tablespoon toasted peanuts, chopped

1 Put the ¼ cup boiling water and tamarind pulp into a heatproof bowl and stir to combine, squashing the pulp to dissolve. Add the brown sugar, fish sauce, peanut oil, tomato paste, soy sauce, and chili flakes and whisk well, then set aside.

2 Put the rice noodles into a large heatproof bowl and cover with boiling water. Set aside for about 5 minutes until just softened, then drain. The noodles will cook some more when added to the wok, so don't soak them for too long at this stage.

3 Heat 1 teaspoon of the extra peanut oil in a large wok, swirl the oil to coat the wok, then add the beaten egg and swirl the wok to make a thin crepe. Cook on one side only and remove as soon as the egg is set, then roll up the crepe and slice into thin strips. Set aside.

4 Heat the remaining teaspoon of oil in the wok. Add the garlic, ginger, and onion and sauté over high heat for 2–3 minutes, or until the onion softens. Add the chicken and sauté for another 2–3 minutes until browned, breaking up any large lumps as you go, then pour in the tamarind sauce. Stir to coat the chicken and allow the sauce to caramelize a little, then add the drained rice noodles, cabbage, snow peas and scallions and cook briefly until heated through.

5 Add the bean sprouts, cilantro, lime juice, and sliced crepe, toss gently to combine. Serve immediately, topped with the peanuts.

Serves 4

Marinated steamed fish

When making Chimichurri, I sometimes substitute the coriander for another herb that complements whatever I'm making. If serving it with lamb, I often use mint, or tarragon if I'm serving it with chicken. In this recipe, oregano makes a nice alternative to the coriander.

2 cod or mackerel fish steaks
2 tablespoons **Chimichurri**, plus extra,
    to serve (recipe page 169)
1 bay leaf
salt and black pepper, to taste

1 Place the fish into a glass or non-reactive bowl and coat each side with the Chimichurri. Cover the bowl and set aside to marinate for 20 minutes.

2 Bring a large saucepan of water to a boil, add the bay leaf, then reduce the heat and bring the water to a low simmer. Place the fish steaks into a greased steamer basket and carefully set over the hot water. Cover tightly and steam the fish for 8–10 minutes, depending on the thickness of the steaks. The fish is cooked when the flesh flakes with a fork.

3 Season with salt and black pepper. Serve with **Vegetable chili** (recipe page 97) and brown rice and offer extra Chimichurri separately.

Serves 2

Corned beef with white sauce

I know corned beef is a bit old fashioned but I love it — don't tell anyone!

3 lb 8 oz piece extra lean, corned beef
1 large white onion, peeled
1 bay leaf
1 teaspoon peppercorns
2 cups **White sauce** (recipe page 169)
1 handful flat-leaf (Italian) parsley,
    chopped

1 Remove the corned beef from its plastic bag and rinse under cold water. Place into a large saucepan or stockpot, then add the onion, bay leaf, peppercorns, and enough cold water to cover the meat by 1¼ inches.

2 Cover the pan and bring to a boil over high heat, then reduce the temperature to very low and simmer for about 2 hours, or until the meat is very tender. Remove the saucepan from the heat but leave the meat to sit in the poaching liquid for another 20 minutes before carving.

3 To serve, drain the corned beef and carve into thick slices. Divide among serving plates and serve drizzled with the White sauce and sprinkled with parsley. Serve with steamed vegetables such as potato, pumpkin (winter squash), carrots, and cauliflower, and **Caraway-spiced red cabbage** (recipe page 67) on the side.

Serves 6–8

Tip: *Corned beef cooks beautifully in the pressure cooker in about 1 hour.*

Apricot chicken

Served with brown rice and broccolini, this is always popular with our six-year-old.

1 tablespoon olive oil
2 white onions, chopped
2 teaspoons crushed garlic
1 lb 10 oz boneless, skinless chicken
    thighs, trimmed of excess fat, cut into
    large pieces
½ cup white wine
9 oz sweet potato, peeled and chopped
1¾ cup apricot nectar
1 cup **Chicken broth** (recipe page 168)
2 tablespoons tomato paste
    (concentrated purée)
salt and pepper, to taste

1 In a casserole dish with a lid, heat the oil and sauté the onions and garlic for 5 minutes, or until softened. Increase the heat, add the chicken to the dish and brown well. Pour in the wine and stir to scrape up the brown residue on the bottom of the dish, then add the sweet potato.

2 In a small bowl, whisk together the apricot nectar, broth, and tomato paste, then pour into the casserole dish and stir well. Cover and simmer over low heat for 30 minutes, or until the chicken is tender.

3 Using a large slotted spoon, remove the chicken to a clean bowl. Using a hand-held blender, purée the ingredients left in the casserole dish, thinning with a little extra water if required. Return the chicken to the dish to heat through, and season to taste with salt and pepper before serving.

Serves 6

Vegetable chili

This is one of those recipes that I never seem to make the same way twice, as I modify the beans, vegetables, and fire depending on what's in the kitchen and who I'm cooking it for. A day or two in the refrigerator mellows the flavors nicely.

1 red onion, chopped
1 tablespoon olive oil
2 teaspoons crushed garlic
1 red bell pepper, diced
1 yellow bell pepper, diced
2 teaspoons cayenne pepper, or to taste
1 teaspoon sweet paprika
1 teaspoon ground cumin
2 zucchini, diced
4 yellow pattypan squash, diced
1 carrot, diced
1 Japanese eggplant, diced
2 14-oz cans chopped tomatoes
1 bay leaf
1 cup corn kernels
2 teaspoons unsweetened cocoa powder (yes, cocoa)
14 oz can beans (kidney, cannellini, or black beans), rinsed and drained
salt, to taste

To serve
cooked white or brown rice
sour cream
chopped cilantro leaves

1 In a large saucepan over low heat, cook the onion in the oil until softened. Add the garlic and peppers, stir to coat in the oil, and cook for another few minutes. Increase the heat to medium, add the cayenne pepper, paprika, and cumin and stir until fragrant, then add the zucchini, squash, carrot, and eggplant and stir to coat with the spices.

2 Reduce the heat to low, add the chopped tomatoes, 1 cup water, and the bay leaf, then cover the pan and leave to simmer for about 30 minutes.

3 Stir in the corn, cocoa, and beans, then replace the lid and simmer for another 10 minutes. Season with salt to taste, then serve over rice, topped with a dollop of sour cream and sprinkled with a little cilantro. Serve with **Cheese and onion cornbread** (recipe page 31) if desired.

Serves 6–8

Goulash

Unlike most casseroles, which benefit from a day or two in the refrigerator, this one is at its best the day it's made, as the caraway loses some of its flavor with time. Alternatively, stir in another teaspoon of caraway seeds when reheating the casserole.

4-5 oz center-cut bacon, chopped
⅓ cup vegetable oil
3 teaspoons crushed garlic
2 leeks, white part only, washed and
    sliced
1 red bell pepper, seeds and membrane
    discarded, diced
3 lb 8 oz blade or chuck steak, trimmed
    and cubed
2 tablespoons sweet paprika
2 teaspoons caraway seeds
¼ cup red wine vinegar
¼ cup tomato paste
    (concentrated purée)
2 cups beef broth
12 fl oz bottle beer
2 generous teaspoons cornstarch, for
    thickening (optional)
½ teaspoon salt (optional)

1 In a large heavy-based saucepan, cook the bacon in a little of the oil until starting to brown, then remove to a heatproof bowl. In the same pan, heat more of the oil and sauté the garlic, leeks, and pepper for 5 minutes, or until softened. Remove to the bowl with the bacon.

2 Add the remaining oil to the pan, increase the heat to high and cook the meat in batches until well browned. Remove the cooked meat to the bowl with the bacon. Reduce the heat and add the paprika and caraway seeds, stirring until fragrant, then add the vinegar, tomato paste, broth, and beer. Stir well to combine, scraping all the brown residue from the bottom of the pan, and bring to a boil. Reduce the heat, return the meat and vegetables to the pan, then cover and simmer for about 1½ hours, depending on the cut of meat used, until fork-tender.

3 If you prefer a thicker gravy, remove about 1 tablespoon of the liquid to a small bowl and stir in the cornstarch until smooth. Increase the heat and stir the cornstarch mixture back into the casserole until it boils and thickens. Add salt and then season to taste with more salt and pepper. Serve the goulash with mashed potatoes and steamed peas and carrots.

Serves 6

Barbecue ribs

Prepare ahead for this sauce, as it benefits from a day or two mellowing in the refrigerator and it also doesn't hurt to marinate the boiled ribs in the sauce overnight before barbecuing. Allow about six ribs per person, more if no one's looking, and choose racks that are on the smaller side and lighter colored, as the larger ones often have an overly strong flavor.

2 tablespoons olive oil

1 large red onion, chopped

3 teaspoons crushed garlic

1 teaspoon ground coriander

½ teaspoon cayenne pepper, or to taste

½ teaspoon sweet paprika

⅓ cup firmly packed brown sugar

½ cup white wine

1½ cups tomato passata (puréed tomatoes)

¼ cup cider vinegar

2 tablespoons Dijon mustard

1 tablespoon Worcestershire sauce

1 tablespoon soy sauce

1 tablespoon fish sauce

salt and freshly ground black pepper, to taste

approximately 3 racks American-style baby pork ribs

1 In a large saucepan or stockpot, heat the oil over low heat, then add the onion and cook for 5–8 minutes, or until softened. Stir in the garlic, coriander, cayenne pepper, paprika, and sugar and cook for a few more minutes until fragrant and the sauce is bubbling.

2 Pour in the wine and scrape up all the brown pieces on the bottom of the pan, then add the rest of the ingredients, except the pork ribs, and season with salt and freshly ground black pepper. Mix together well, then cover and cook over low heat for about 20 minutes, or until slightly thickened. Allow the sauce to cool a little, then pour into a glass or stainless-steel bowl, cover, and refrigerate for at least 24 hours.

3 Cut the racks of ribs into smaller portions and place into a large stockpot with a lid. Add enough water to cover, bring to a boil, cover and simmer very gently for 1 hour.

4 Heat the grill. Drain the ribs and pat dry with paper towel, then brush generously with the sauce and grill for about 10 minutes, or until well browned and fragrant, basting liberally with more sauce. Serve the ribs hot off the grill with the remaining sauce, **Asian-style coleslaw** (recipe page 64) on the side and with finger bowls and hand towels nearby.

Serves 6

Chicken with prosciutto and mushrooms in mustard and caper sauce

1 lb 8 oz boneless, skinless chicken
    thighs, trimmed of excess fat,
    chopped into smaller pieces
2 teaspoons crushed garlic
2 tablespoons olive oil
6 oz button mushrooms, chopped
3-4 oz prosciutto, chopped
½ cup white wine
1 cup **Chicken broth** (recipe page 168)
¼ cup whipping cream
2 teaspoons cornstarch
1 teaspoon whole grain mustard
2 tablespoons chopped flat-leaf (Italian)
    parsley
1 generous tablespoon capers, rinsed
salt and pepper, to taste

1 In a large frying pan with a lid, sauté the chicken and garlic in the olive oil for 5 minutes, or until well browned, then remove to a bowl. Add the mushrooms and prosciutto to the pan and cook for 2–3 minutes, or until the prosciutto starts to brown.

2 Add the wine and stir to loosen the brown pieces on the bottom of the pan, then return the chicken to the pan, add the broth and bring to a boil. Reduce the heat, cover, and simmer over low heat for 15–20 minutes, or until the chicken is tender.

3 In a small bowl, combine the cream and cornstarch and stir until smooth, then stir in the mustard, parsley, and capers.

4 When the chicken is tender, add the cream mixture and stir until the sauce thickens slightly. Season to taste with salt and pepper and serve with mashed potatoes and steamed green beans.

Serves 4

Meat loaf

2 oz prosciutto (about 6 slices)
1 red onion, chopped
½ cup grated parmesan cheese
2 eggs
1 tablespoon tomato paste
    (concentrated purée)
1 tablespoon Worcestershire sauce
1 teaspoon crushed garlic
1 large handful flat-leaf (Italian) parsley,
    chopped
½ teaspoon dried Italian herbs
½ teaspoon salt
½ cup gluten-free fresh breadcrumbs
1 lb 8 oz minced (ground) beef
10 oz minced (ground) lamb
1 cup grated zucchini

Gravy
1 tablespoon cornstarch
1 tablespoon tomato paste
    (concentrated purée)
salt and pepper, to taste

1 Line a large 9 x 5 x 3-inch loaf pan with plastic wrap, leaving the plastic overhanging at each end (enough to cover the loaf).

2 Place the prosciutto, onion, parmesan, eggs, tomato paste, Worcestershire sauce, garlic, parsley, dried herbs, and salt into the bowl of a food processor and pulse to form a thick paste. Spoon the paste into a large mixing bowl, then add the breadcrumbs, beef, lamb, and grated zucchini.

3 Using clean hands, squeeze and mix the ingredients until fully combined. Transfer the mixture into the pan, pushing down firmly to make a solid loaf. Fold over the excess plastic wrap to cover and then refrigerate for a few hours for the flavors to develop.

4 When ready to bake, preheat the oven to 350°F and grease a large baking pan.

5 Uncover the meat loaf and flip it over into the baking pan, then remove the loaf pan and discard the plastic wrap. Bake the meat loaf for about 70 minutes, or until well browned and the juices run clear when the loaf is pierced with a skewer. Wrap in a double layer of foil to keep warm while you make the gravy.

6 To make the gravy, pour off all but 1 tablespoon of fat from the baking pan, then stir in the cornstarch and cook over low heat for 1–2 minutes. Pour in 1½ cups water, stirring to loosen the tasty brown bits on the bottom of the pan, then continue stirring until the sauce thickens. Blend in the tomato paste, season with salt and pepper, and strain into a gravy boat.

7 Carve the meat loaf into thick slices and serve smothered in gravy, with mashed potatoes, baked pumpkin (winter squash) and peas, and a nice cold gluten-free beer on the side.

Serves 6–8

Sage and prosciutto pork fillet

1 cup sage leaves
2 generous teaspoons Dijon mustard
1 teaspoon crushed garlic
about 1 tablespoon olive oil
2 x 1 lb–1 lb 8 oz pork tenderloin fillets
24 thin slices prosciutto
½ cup **Chicken broth** (recipe page 168)
Caraway-spiced red cabbage, to serve
   (recipe page 67)

1 Preheat the oven to 350°F and lightly grease a baking dish.

2 Put the sage, mustard, and garlic in a food processor and chop briefly. With the motor running, add about 1 tablespoon of olive oil, or enough to form a paste. Rub the paste evenly over the pork.

3 Lay half the prosciutto out on the work surface, leaving it on the plastic sheet from the delicatessen if possible; otherwise, place overlapping slices onto a piece of plastic wrap. Place one of the pork pieces onto the prosciutto slices, tucking under the thin end of the pork so that it's of a fairly even shape. Using the plastic as a guide, wrap the prosciutto around the pork. Repeat with the remaining prosciutto and pork.

4 Place the pork into the dish, seam side down, and bake for about 25 minutes. Remove from the oven, wrap tightly in foil and allow the meat to rest for 10 minutes before slicing.

5 Place the baking dish onto the stovetop and deglaze the pan with the broth to make a light gravy.

6 To serve, place two or three slices of pork onto a plate, along with some cabbage. Drizzle with a little of the gravy and serve with mashed sweet potato on the side.

Serves 6

Baked salmon with dill

1¾ oz (3½ tablespoons) butter
2 tablespoons finely chopped dill
1 tablespoon grated lemon zest
1 tablespoon lemon juice
4–6 salmon fillets

1 Preheat the oven to 425°F. Line a roasting pan with lightly greased foil.

2 Combine the butter, dill, lemon zest, and juice in a small saucepan over low heat and stir until the butter is melted.

3 Place the salmon fillets into the prepared pan and brush generously with the herbed butter. Depending on the thickness of the fillets, bake for about 12 minutes, or until cooked to your liking. Serve drizzled with the cooking juices, and with **Spinach and lemon pilaf** (recipe page 51) on the side.

Serves 4–6

Roast chicken with stuffing and gravy

3 lb 8 oz whole chicken
olive oil
freshly ground salt or sea salt

Stuffing
4 slices gluten-free bread
1 scallion, including the green stem,
    peeled and chopped
1 oz prosciutto, chopped
2 tablespoons chopped flat-leaf (Italian)
    parsley
½ teaspoon dried mixed herbs
½ teaspoon crushed garlic
2 tablespoons lentils, rinsed and drained
1 tablespoon olive oil
salt and pepper, to taste

Gravy
1 tablespoon cornstarch
½ cup white wine
1½ cups **Chicken broth** (recipe page 168)
¼ teaspoon soy sauce
salt and pepper, to taste

1 Preheat the oven to 350°F.

2 To make the stuffing, put the bread, scallion, prosciutto, parsley, dried herbs, and garlic in the bowl of a food processor and process to form lentil-sized crumbs. Put into a bowl and stir in the lentils and oil. Season with salt and pepper.

3 Wash the chicken inside and out and pat dry with a paper towel. Using clean hands, squeeze small handfuls of stuffing into balls and pack into the chicken cavity, then skewer the opening closed, rub a little olive oil onto the skin, and sprinkle with ground salt.

4 Tie the legs together with kitchen string, place the chicken into a large enamel baking pan, tucking the wings under the body. Allow 25 minutes baking time for each 1 lb (approximate) of chicken, basting twice with the cooking juices. When the skin is golden brown and the juice runs clear when the thigh is pierced with a skewer, wrap the chicken tightly in a double layer of foil and leave to rest for 10 minutes.

5 Meanwhile, make the gravy. Pour off all but 1 tablespoon of fat from the baking pan and place the pan over medium heat on the stovetop. Sprinkle in the cornstarch and stir to make a paste, scraping up the brown pieces on the bottom of the pan as you go. Pour in the wine and stir until smooth, then reduce the heat, add the broth and continue stirring until the gravy boils and thickens. Add the soy sauce to deepen the color and flavor, then season to taste with salt and pepper. Strain into a gravy boat and reheat in the microwave before serving if necessary.

6 To serve, cut the chicken into large pieces and remove all of the stuffing from the cavity with a spoon. Divide the chicken among the dinner plates along with a generous spoonful of stuffing on the side, and pour over the gravy.

Serves 6

Osso bucco

2 tablespoons olive oil
4 lb 8 oz veal shank pieces
2 carrots, diced
1 onion, diced
1 teaspoon crushed garlic
1 cup red wine
1 cup tomato passata (puréed tomatoes)
1 cup veal or beef broth
1 tablespoon tomato paste
   (concentrated purée)
2 thyme sprigs
1 bay leaf
1 long rosemary sprig
1 strip lemon zest, without pith
salt and pepper, to taste

Gremolata
2 large handfuls flat-leaf (Italian) parsley,
   chopped
1 tablespoon finely grated lemon zest
1 teaspoon crushed garlic
2 teaspoons rinsed and chopped
   baby capers

1 Heat the olive oil in a large casserole dish over high heat and brown the veal pieces on all sides in two batches. Remove to a bowl. Reduce the heat, add the carrots, onion, and garlic to the dish and sauté for about 5 minutes, or until the vegetables soften. Remove to the bowl with the veal.

2 Pour the wine into the dish, stirring to release the brown bits from the bottom. Return the meat and vegetables to the casserole and pour over the tomato passata, broth, and tomato paste. Mix well.

3 Tie the thyme, bay leaf, rosemary, and lemon zest together with kitchen string and submerge it in the middle of the sauce, then cover with a lid. Bring to a boil, then reduce the heat to low and cook for 1½–2 hours, or until the meat is very tender. Check occasionally to ensure there is enough liquid, adding a little more broth if necessary.

4 Meanwhile, make the gremolata. In a small bowl, combine the parsley, lemon zest, garlic, and capers. Mix well.

5 When the osso bucco is ready to serve, season to taste with salt and pepper and discard the bunch of herbs. Place one or two veal pieces onto each plate along with some gravy. Top with a teaspoon of gremolata, and pass the remainder at the table. Serve with **Green pea risotto** (recipe page 74) on the side.

Serves 4

Tip: *If you have one, osso bucco cooks beautifully in a pressure cooker in about 25 minutes.*

Braised lamb shanks

12 French shallots, unpeeled
1 tablespoon olive oil
4 lamb shanks
2 carrots, diced
2 celery stalks, diced
2 teaspoons crushed garlic
2 cups red wine
2 tablespoons tomato paste
   (concentrated purée)
1 long rosemary sprig or 1 teaspoon
   dried rosemary
1 bay leaf
1 thyme sprig or ½ teaspoon dried
   thyme
salt and pepper, to taste

1 Preheat the oven to 300°F.

2 In a small saucepan, boil the shallots in water for a couple of minutes, then drain. When cool enough to handle, cut off the root end and squeeze out the shallot.

3 Heat the olive oil in a large casserole dish over high heat, add the lamb shanks and brown on all sides. Remove to a heatproof bowl.

4 Add the shallots, carrots, celery, and garlic to the casserole dish and sauté for 2–3 minutes, or until starting to brown, then remove to the bowl with the lamb shanks.

5 Pour in the red wine and stir to scrape up the brown residue on the bottom of the dish. Add 1 cup water, the tomato paste, rosemary, bay leaf, and thyme and stir to combine. Return the lamb and vegetables to the dish, stir again to combine, then cover and bake for 1½–2 hours, or until fork-tender, turning the lamb shanks twice during cooking.

6 Season to taste with salt and pepper and serve in large bowls with mashed potatoes, steamed green beans, and lots of gravy.

Serves 4

SOMETHING SWEET

Occasionally people assume that because I follow a gluten-free diet I eat only low-fat, low-sugar, healthy food — they are greatly mistaken . . .

Hazelnut buttons

1 cup **Rice flour blend** (recipe page 9)
¼ cup sweet rice flour
½ teaspoon baking powder
½ teaspoon xanthan gum
2 tablespoons unsweetened cocoa
    powder
1 tablespoon ground hazelnuts
3½ oz (7 tablespoons) butter, softened
1 tablespoon coconut oil
½ cup superfine sugar
1 egg

Hazelnut cream
⅔ cup confectioners' sugar, sifted
1¾ oz (3½ tablespoons) butter, softened
⅓ cup hazelnut spread
½–1 tablespoon milk

1 Preheat the oven to 325°F. Line two baking sheets with parchment paper.

2 Sift the Rice flour blend, sweet rice flour, baking powder, xanthan gum, cocoa, and ground hazelnuts into a bowl, breaking up any lumps with the back of a spoon.

3 In a separate bowl and using electric beaters, beat the butter, coconut oil, and sugar together until light and creamy, then add the egg and beat until well combined. Stir in the dry ingredients with a large spoon until completely mixed.

4 Spoon the mixture into a cookie press or piping bag fitted with a large round nozzle and pipe 1¼-inch rounds onto the prepared baking sheets. Allow a little room for spreading.

5 Bake for about 8 minutes, swapping the trays around halfway through baking time. Rest the cookies on the trays for a few minutes before transferring onto wire racks to cool. Repeat with the remaining batter.

6 To make the hazelnut cream, put the confectioners' sugar, butter, and hazelnut spread into a food processor and process until smooth. Gradually add the milk, using only enough to make the mixture a good consistency for piping. Place the cream into a piping bag fitted with a decorative nozzle and pipe onto the cooled cookies.

Makes about 48 cookies

Cookie press cookies

A cookie press is the gadget you've seen at kitchenware shops that makes those pretty European-style Christmas cookies. Usually packaged as a set, including several cookie discs and a selection of icing tips, it's ideal for dispensing small amounts of even-sized dough or batter. I find it such a handy thing I now have two.

1 cup ground almonds
¾ cup **Rice flour blend** (recipe page 9)
⅓ cup sweet rice flour
1 teaspoon pumpkin pie spice
¼ teaspoon xanthan gum
pinch of salt
1¾ oz (3½ tablespoons) butter, softened
¼ cup coconut oil
½ cup superfine sugar
1 egg
½ teaspoon vanilla extract

1 Preheat the oven to 325°F. Line two baking sheets with parchment paper. Fit a decorative disc into a cookie press.

2 Sift the almonds, Rice flour blend, sweet rice flour, pumpkin pie spice, xanthan gum, and salt into a bowl, discarding any larger pieces of almond as these may clog the cookie press. Whisk well to combine.

3 In a separate bowl and using electric beaters, beat the butter, coconut oil, and sugar until creamy, then add the egg and vanilla and beat again. Stir in the dry ingredients until fully mixed.

4 Spoon the dough into the cookie press and press them onto the prepared baking sheets. Bake for about 8 minutes, or until lightly browned. Rest the cookies on the trays for a few minutes before transferring onto wire racks to cool. Repeat with the remaining dough.

Makes about 48 cookies

Rum and raisin cookies

1 cup raisins
¼ cup dark rum
4½ oz (9 tablespoons) butter, softened
¾ cup firmly packed brown sugar
1 egg
1¾ cups **Rice flour blend**
   (recipe page 9)
1 teaspoon baking powder
½ teaspoon xanthan gum
6 oz dark chocolate, melted, to decorate

1 In a small non-metallic bowl, combine the raisins and rum and leave to soak while you assemble the rest of the ingredients.

2 Preheat the oven to 350°F. Line two baking sheets with parchment paper. Drain the raisins, reserving the rum.

3 In a bowl and using electric beaters, cream the butter and sugar until fluffy, then add the egg and reserved rum and beat well. Stir in the Rice flour blend, baking powder, and xanthan gum until well mixed, then stir in the raisins.

4 Roll generous teaspoons of the mixture into balls and place onto the prepared trays, spacing them apart to allow room for spreading, and flatten slightly with a fork. Bake for 10–12 minutes, or until lightly browned.

5 Spread the melted chocolate over the cookies while they are still warm, then remove to a wire rack and allow to cool completely.

Makes about 30 cookies

Mixed nut bars

1 cup salted and roasted mixed nuts
3½ oz (7 tablespoons) butter, cut into
    cubes
1 tablespoon coconut oil
⅓ cup confectioners' sugar, sifted
1 teaspoon vanilla extract
1 egg
¾ cup white rice flour
¼ cup sweet rice flour
1 tablespoon pure maple syrup
2 teaspoons superfine sugar

1 Preheat the oven to 350°F. Line a 11 x 7-inch rectangular baking pan with a long sheet of parchment paper, leaving the paper overhanging at each end.

2 Put the mixed nuts into the bowl of a food processor and process until roughly chopped. This will make it easier to cut the finished bars. Remove to a bowl.

3 Put the butter, coconut oil, confectioners' sugar, vanilla, egg, and flours into the bowl of the food processor and process until smooth. Spread the mixture evenly over the base of the prepared pan.

4 Combine the chopped nuts, maple syrup, and superfine sugar, stir until fully mixed, then press the nut mixture evenly onto the base. Bake for 20–25 minutes, or until nicely browned, turning the pan around in the oven after 10 minutes.

5 Remove from the oven and allow to firm up in the pan for a few minutes before gently lifting onto a wire rack to cool. Cut into pieces when fully cooled.

Makes about 21 bars

Brownies

This is a great recipe for the budding chef in your house.

7 oz packaged gluten-free cookies
   (shortbread or rice flour based,
   crumbly in texture)
½ cup macadamia nuts
5½ oz (11 tablespoons) butter
⅔ cup superfine sugar
½ cup unsweetened cocoa powder,
   sifted
2 eggs, lightly beaten

1 Preheat the oven to 325°F. Line a 11 x 7-inch rectangular baking pan with a long sheet of parchment paper, leaving the paper overhanging at each end.

2 Place the cookies into the bowl of a food processor and process to form fine crumbs. Remove to a large mixing bowl. Place the nuts into the food processor and process until coarsely chopped, then remove to the bowl with the crumbs and stir to combine.

3 Put the butter, sugar, and cocoa into a small saucepan and stir over low heat until melted. Remove from the heat and stir in the crumbs, then add the beaten eggs and mix thoroughly.

4 Spoon the batter evenly into the prepared pan, smooth the top and bake for about 15 minutes, turning the pan around in the oven after 10 minutes.

5 Allow to firm up in the pan for 10 minutes, then lift out and carefully slide off the parchment paper and onto a wire rack to cool completely. When fully cooled, cut into squares or bars.

Makes about 21 pieces

Spicy fruit pillows

Both the pastry and fruit filling for these cookies can be prepared in advance and then assembled just before baking

1 quantity **Sweet short-crust pastry**
(recipe page 170)

Filling
1½ cups raisins
1 cup pitted dates
½ cup currants
2 tablespoons marmalade
grated zest of 1 orange
1 teaspoon ground cinnamon
½ teaspoon ground cloves
½ teaspoon freshly grated nutmeg

1 To make the filling, put the raisins, dates, and currants into the bowl of a food processor and pulse until finely chopped. Add the marmalade, orange zest, and spices and pulse until well combined. Cover and chill until needed.

2 Preheat the oven to 325°F. Line two baking sheets with parchment paper.

3 Place half of the pastry (one disc) onto a large sheet of parchment paper, cover with another sheet of parchment paper, and roll out into a rectangular shape about ⅛–¼ inch thick. Flip the pastry over and smooth out any creases on the back, then remove the top sheet of parchment paper.

4 Using wet hands, roll a small amount of the fruit filling into a long log and place it just inside one edge of the pastry. Using the parchment paper to roll, enclose the fruit with pastry and then cut the roll away from the large piece of pastry. Cut the log into 1¼–1½-inch pieces and roll gently to seal the seam and flatten the ends slightly. Repeat with the remaining pastry and fruit filling.

5 Place onto the prepared baking sheets and bake for 15–18 minutes, or until lightly browned. Remove to a wire rack to cool.

Makes about 24 cookies

Lamingtons

The amounts I've given for icing and coconut will probably be more than you'll need, but because lamingtons are so messy to make I've included an allowance for spills, drips and finger licking.

1 recipe **Genoise sponge cake** batter
    (recipe page 143)
4 cups confectioners' sugar, sifted
⅓ cup unsweetened cocoa powder,
    sifted
1¾ oz (3½ tablespoons) butter, melted
½ cup milk
2 cups desiccated coconut
    (unsweetened)

1 Preheat the oven to 350°F. Grease and line the base of a 11 x 7-inch rectangular baking pan with parchment paper.

2 Make up the Genoise sponge cake batter, pour into the prepared pan, and bake for about 15 minutes, or until the sponge cake springs back when gently pressed in the middle. Allow the cake to firm up in the pan for 5 minutes, then turn out onto a wire rack, remove the parchment paper and leave to cool upside down. When the cake is fully cooled, cut into 18 even pieces.

3 In a heatproof bowl over gently simmering water, combine the confectioners' sugar, cocoa, melted butter, and milk and stir until smooth. Turn off the heat but leave the bowl over the hot water.

4 Place the coconut onto a large sheet of parchment paper next to a wire rack. Using a small fork to hold the cake, dip one piece of cake at a time into the chocolate icing, turning it until completely covered. Hold the lamington above the bowl for a moment to allow the excess icing to run off, then drop into the coconut and turn to coat on all sides. Place the lamington onto a wire rack to set. Repeat with the remaining cake, icing, and coconut.

Makes 18

Cupcakes

1 cup **Rice flour blend** (recipe page 9)
¼ cup sweet rice flour
1 teaspoon baking powder
½ teaspoon baking soda
¼ teaspoon xanthan gum
¼ teaspoon salt
4½ oz (9 tablespoons) butter, softened
1 tablespoon coconut oil
⅔ cup sugar
2 eggs
¼ cup plain Greek-style yogurt
1 teaspoon vanilla extract

Butter cream

3½ oz (7 tablespoons) butter, softened
1½ cups confectioners' sugar, sifted
1 tablespoon milk
¼ teaspoon vanilla extract
food coloring

1 Preheat the oven to 325°F. Place silicone cupcake molds onto baking sheets or place paper cases into two 12-cup cupcake tins.

2 In a bowl, combine the Rice flour blend, sweet rice flour, baking powder, baking soda, xanthan gum, and salt and whisk to combine.

3 In a separate bowl and using electric beaters, beat the butter, coconut oil, and sugar until pale and creamy, then add the eggs one at a time, beating well after each addition. Stir in half the dry ingredients until fully mixed, then add the yogurt and vanilla. Stir to combine, then add the rest of the dry ingredients and stir just until fully incorporated.

4 Divide the batter evenly between the muffin cups, filling each cup about three-quarters full, and bake for 13–15 minutes, or until the cakes have risen and are evenly browned, turning the trays around in the oven halfway through cooking. Allow the cakes to firm up for about 8 minutes, then turn out onto a wire rack to cool.

5 Meanwhile, make the butter cream. Using electric beaters, beat the butter until pale and fluffy, then add the confectioners' sugar, milk, and vanilla and mix well. Add a little more milk if necessary to achieve a good spreading consistency, then stir in a few drops of food coloring. When the cupcakes are completely cooled, decorate with the butter cream.

Makes 16–18 cupcakes

Chocolate sheet cake

This is a good recipe if you're looking for a party cake. I bake it in my lasagna dish, which is just the right size. For a mocha version, replace the water with a cup of strong brewed coffee.

4½ oz (9 tablespoons) butter
¾ cup unsweetened cocoa powder, sifted
2 cups **Rice flour blend** (recipe page 9)
1½ cups superfine sugar
2 teaspoons baking powder
1 teaspoon baking soda
1 teaspoon xanthan gum
½ teaspoon salt
½ cup plain Greek-style yogurt
2 eggs
1 teaspoon vanilla extract

Chocolate frosting
1¾ oz (3½ tablespoons) butter, softened
1¼ cups powdered chocolate icing/frosting mix
1 tablespoon milk

1 Preheat the oven to 325°F. Grease and line the base of a 9 x 13 x 2-inch rectangular baking dish with parchment paper.

2 In a small saucepan over low heat, stir the butter, cocoa, and 1 cup water until smooth. Remove from the heat and allow to cool.

3 In a bowl, combine the Rice flour blend, sugar, baking powder, baking soda, xanthan gum, and salt. Stir in the cocoa mixture.

4 In a separate bowl, whisk together the yogurt, eggs, and vanilla, then beat into the flour and cocoa mixture until well blended.

5 Pour the batter into the prepared dish and bake for 35 minutes, or until a skewer inserted in the middle comes out clean. Allow the cake to firm up in the dish for 7–8 minutes, then turn out onto a wire rack, remove the parchment paper and allow to cool, right side up.

6 Meanwhile, to make the chocolate frosting, combine the butter, chocolate icing mixture, and milk in the bowl of a food processor and process until smooth, adding a little extra milk if necessary to achieve a good spreading consistency. When the cake is fully cooled, decorate with the chocolate frosting, as desired.

Serves 12–16

Coco-banana-nut cake

A bundt pan is perfect for this cake.

1 cup **Rice flour blend** (recipe page 9)
1 cup desiccated coconut (unsweetened)
½ cup superfine sugar
½ cup brazil nuts, ground
2 teaspoons baking powder
½ teaspoon xanthan gum
1 overripe banana, mashed
1 cup coconut milk
1 egg
½ teaspoon vanilla extract
2 tablespoons shredded coconut, toasted

Coconut icing
¾ oz (1½ tablespoons) butter, softened
1 cup confectioners' sugar, sifted
2–3 tablespoons coconut milk

1 Preheat the oven to 325°F. Grease a 8-inch bundt pan or ring mold.

2 In a bowl, combine the Rice flour blend, coconut, sugar, ground nuts, baking powder, and xanthan gum and whisk to combine.

3 In a separate bowl, combine the mashed banana, coconut milk, egg, and vanilla and mix well, then add to the dry ingredients. Stir to combine thoroughly, then pour into the prepared pan.

4 Bake for about 35 minutes, or until evenly browned, turning the pan around in the oven after 20 minutes. Allow the cake to firm up in the pan for 10 minutes, then turn out to cool, right side up, on a wire rack.

5 To make the coconut icing, put the butter and confectioners' sugar in a small bowl. Add enough of the coconut milk to make a smooth and fairly runny icing. When the cake is fully cooled, drizzle over the coconut icing and sprinkle with toasted coconut.

Lemon poppy seed cake

1½ cups **Rice flour blend** (recipe
    page 9)
1 tablespoon poppy seeds
2 teaspoons baking powder
¾ teaspoon xanthan gum
½ teaspoon baking soda
½ teaspoon salt
4½ oz (9 tablespoons) butter, softened
finely grated zest of 1 lemon
⅔ cup superfine sugar
2 eggs
1 egg white
½ cup plain Greek-style yogurt
⅓ cup lemon juice

Lemon icing
1 cup confectioners' sugar, sifted
1 tablespoon lemon juice
1 tablespoon finely grated lemon zest

1 Preheat the oven to 325°F. Grease a 10-inch bundt pan or
ring mold.

2 Sift the Rice flour blend, poppy seeds, baking powder, xanthan
gum, baking soda, and salt over a sheet of parchment paper.

3 In a separate bowl and using electric beaters, beat the butter,
lemon zest, and sugar until creamy, then add the eggs and egg
white one at a time, beating well after each addition.

4 Stir in half the dry ingredients until combined, then add the yogurt
and lemon juice and stir again. Add the rest of the dry ingredients
and mix well.

5 Spoon the batter into the prepared pan and smooth the top. Bake
for 20–25 minutes, or until risen and browned. Allow the cake to
firm up in the pan for a few minutes, then turn out onto a wire rack
to cool, right side up.

6 To make the lemon icing, combine the confectioners' sugar, lemon
juice, and 1 teaspoon water in a bowl and mix until smooth. Drizzle
the icing over the cooled cake and sprinkle with lemon zest.

Serves 8

Rich fruit cake

It can be quite difficult gauging when a fruit cake is completely cooked through, but I've found a large springform ring mold shortens the baking time and removes the soggy middle dilemma. If possible, source your dried fruit and nuts from a specialist retailer, as the box of mixed fruit from the supermarket doesn't do a fruit cake justice. Check the Internet for mail order services. Be aware that you must prepare the dried fruit and nuts for this cake a day or two ahead of baking the cake.

2 cups golden raisins

⅔ cup currants

⅔ cup pitted dates, chopped

heaped 1 cup dried cranberries

½ cup dried blueberries

½ cup mixed citrus peel

⅓ cup blanched almonds, chopped

⅓ cup brazil nuts, chopped

⅓ cup pecan nuts, chopped

2 tablespoons marmalade

finely grated zest of 1 lemon

finely grated zest of 1 orange

½ cup brandy

1 cup white rice flour

1 cup soy flour

1 teaspoon baking soda

1 teaspoon pumpkin pie spice

1 teaspoon xanthan gum

6½ oz (13 tablespoons) butter, softened

1 cup brown sugar

4 eggs

1 In a large bowl, combine the dried fruit, nuts, marmalade, lemon and orange zests, and brandy and stir well to combine. Cover the bowl and set aside for a day or two, stirring the fruit occasionally.

2 When ready to bake, preheat the oven to 300°F. Grease and line the base of a 10-inch springform ring mold.

3 Combine the rice flour, soy flour, baking soda, pumpkin pie spice, and xanthan gum in a bowl and whisk to combine.

4 In a large mixing bowl and using electric beaters, beat the butter and sugar until creamy. Add the eggs one at a time, mixing well after each addition, then add the dry ingredients and beat again. Using a large spoon, stir in the soaked fruit until evenly distributed.

5 Spoon the batter into the prepared ring mold and bake for about 1¼ hours, or until the cake is a rich brown on top and starting to pull away from the side of the pan. Remove the pan from the oven, wrap in a clean dish towel, and leave the cake in the pan until fully cooled.

6 To unmold the cake, run a knife around the side of the pan, invert onto a cutting board, and release the spring. Store the cake wrapped in wax paper and foil but avoid plastic, which makes it sweat, and don't store in the refrigerator, as this tends to make the cake hard.

Genoise sponge cake

3 eggs
2 egg yolks
½ cup superfine sugar
⅔ cup **Rice flour blend** (recipe page 9)
¼ teaspoon xanthan gum
pinch of salt
2¼ oz (4½ tablespoons) butter, melted
    and cooled
1 teaspoon vanilla extract

To serve
1 cup heavy whipping cream
½ teaspoon sifted confectioners' sugar
1 teaspoon vanilla extract
⅔ cup raspberry jam
confectioners' sugar, extra
fresh raspberries (optional)

1 Preheat the oven to 400°F, positioning the rack in the lower third of the oven. Grease and line the bases of two 8-inch round cake pans with parchment paper.

2 Place the eggs, egg yolks, and sugar into a heatproof bowl set over a saucepan of simmering water and whisk until the sugar has dissolved and the mixture is warm. Remove the bowl from the water and beat with an electric mixer on medium speed for 2 minutes, then increase the speed to high and beat for another 3 minutes, or until the mixture is very thick and tripled in volume.

3 Sift the Rice flour blend, xanthan gum, and a pinch of salt over the egg mixture and fold in gently with a rubber spatula. Add the melted butter and vanilla, gently pouring down the side of the bowl, and then continue to fold in until completely incorporated.

4 Divide the mixture between the prepared pans and bake for about 12 minutes, or until evenly browned and pulling away from the side, swapping the pans around after 8 minutes. Remove the pans from the oven and allow the cakes to rest and firm up for a few minutes before turning out onto a wire rack and removing the parchment paper.

5 In a large mixing bowl and using electric beaters, whip the cream, ½ teaspoon confectioners' sugar, and vanilla together until thickened.

6 When the cakes are fully cooled, place one sponge upside down onto a cake plate and spread the raspberry jam over the base, then spread with the cream. Place the other cake on top so the bases are together, and sift the top with the extra icing sugar. Decorate with fresh raspberries if desired.

Serves 8

Truffle nut tart

½ quantity **Sweet short-crust pastry**
(recipe page 170)
1 cup whipping cream
6 oz dark chocolate, chopped
½ cup hazelnut spread
1 cup combined chopped macadamia
nuts and blanched almonds

1 Lightly grease a 14 x 4¼-inch rectangular loose-based tart pan.

2 Place the pastry onto a large sheet of parchment paper, cover with another sheet of parchment paper, and roll out to fit the tart pan. Flip the pastry over and smooth out any creases on the back.

3 Remove the top sheet of parchment paper and carefully ease the pastry into the tart pan, removing the remaining sheet of paper as you go. Run a knife around the top of the pan to cut off the excess pastry and use this to patch any tears or thin spots. Refrigerate the pastry for at least 30 minutes until firm and cold.

4 When ready to bake, preheat the oven to 325°F.

5 Remove the pastry from the refrigerator and prick in a few places with a skewer, then place one sheet of parchment paper back into the pastry shell and fill with pie weights or dried beans. Bake for 10 minutes, then remove the pie weights and parchment paper, turn the pan around and bake for another 15–20 minutes, or until dried and lightly browned all over. Leave the pastry shell in the pan to cool.

6 To make the filling, combine the cream, chocolate, and hazelnut spread in a heatproof bowl. Place the bowl over a saucepan of gently simmering water and stir until melted and smooth. Remove from the heat and refrigerate until the mixture is slightly thickened.

7 Spread the nuts over the cooled pastry shell, then spoon in the chocolate truffle mixture, smooth the top, and refrigerate overnight, or until set. Remove the tart from the refrigerator 20 minutes before required, and serve slices at room temperature.

Serves 8

Tip: *This nut tart keeps perfectly in the refrigerator for up to 4 days.*

Pantry apple pudding

This is a simple cake, made from everyday ingredients, for dessert emergencies.

1 lb 12 oz canned apple slices (plain)
1 teaspoon pumpkin pie spice
3½ oz (7 tablespoons) butter, softened
½ cup brown sugar
2 eggs
⅔ cup **Rice flour blend** (recipe page 9)
¼ cup ground hazelnuts
2 teaspoons baking powder
½ teaspoon xanthan gum
1 tablespoon plain Greek-style yogurt
½ teaspoon vanilla extract

1 Preheat the oven to 325°F. Lightly grease a 8-inch round soufflé dish or deep cake pan.

2 Place the apples and pumpkin pie spice into the prepared dish and toss lightly to mix.

3 In a mixing bowl and using electric beaters, beat the butter and sugar until creamy, then add the eggs one at a time, beating well after each addition. Beat in the Rice flour blend, ground hazelnuts, baking powder, and xanthan gum until fully combined. Add the yogurt and vanilla, beating only until incorporated.

4 Spread the batter over the apples, smooth the top, and bake for 30–35 minutes, or until evenly browned and the cake is cooked through. Serve warm with cream or **Vanilla-bean ice cream** (recipe page 148).

Serves 6

Vanilla-bean ice cream

It's not hard to find gluten-free ice cream but homemade is just so much better.

2 vanilla beans
1⅓ cups milk
4 egg yolks
½ cup superfine sugar
1⅓ cups heavy whipping cream

1 Split the vanilla beans lengthways and place into a saucepan with the milk. Stir over high heat, only until small bubbles start to appear around the edge, then remove the pan from the heat and leave the vanilla beans to steep for 30 minutes. Remove the vanilla beans and scrape out some of the seeds into the milk.

2 Return the pan to the heat and bring the milk to a low simmer.

3 In a heatproof bowl, whisk the egg yolks and sugar until thick and a pale lemon color. While still whisking, slowly pour in the hot milk. Return the custard to the saucepan and cook over very low heat, whisking constantly, until the custard is thick enough to coat the back of a spoon. Don't let the custard boil or it will separate.

4 Remove the pan from the heat and whisk in the cold cream, then strain the custard into a clean bowl, cover and refrigerate overnight.

5 Pour the custard into an ice-cream maker and proceed according to the manufacturer's instructions. Place the ice cream into an airtight container and freeze until firm.

Makes about 2½ cups

Ice cream cones

You will need a special ice cream cone maker to make this recipe. The cones are best eaten the day they are made.

2 eggs
¾ cup confectioners' sugar
¼ teaspoon salt
2 tablespoons coconut oil
½ teaspoon vanilla extract
¾ cup white rice flour
¼ cup sweet rice flour
⅓ cup coconut milk, shaken

1 Preheat an ice cream cone maker.

2 In a bowl, whisk together the eggs, confectioners' sugar, and salt until light in color, then add the coconut oil and vanilla and mix well. Gently whisk in the rice flours, then the coconut milk, and continue whisking until smooth and runny. Add a little more coconut milk if necessary; the mixture should be the consistency of a crepe batter and won't crisp up well if it's too thick.

3 Pour generous tablespoons of batter onto the cone maker and close the lid. Cook according to the manufacturer's instructions, but I find I need to turn my cones over halfway through cooking time to brown evenly.

4 Remove the cooked cone, place onto a paper towel, and gently roll to shape, then hold it together for a minute until set. Don't worry about any gaps in the bottom of the cone, as these can be plugged later with a gluten-free marshmallow or some melted chocolate. Repeat with the remaining batter. Serve with **Vanilla-bean ice cream** (recipe page 148).

Makes 8–10 cones

Balsamic strawberry cheesecake

This cheesecake doesn't set as firmly as a regular cheesecake and, despite the list of ingredients that may indicate otherwise, it's not overly sweet.

1¾ oz dark chocolate, chopped
1¾ oz (3½ tablespoons) butter, chopped
1 tablespoon superfine sugar
1½ cups desiccated coconut,
    unsweetened
1⅔ cups strawberries, quartered
2 tablespoons brown sugar
2 teaspoons balsamic vinegar
9 oz plain cream cheese, softened
½ cup confectioners' sugar, sifted
4½ oz mascarpone cheese
whipped cream, to serve (optional)

1 Grease a 9- or 10-inch round springform pan and line the base with parchment paper.

2 Put the chocolate, butter, and superfine sugar in the top of a double boiler and place over barely simmering water. Stir until melted. Remove from the heat and stir in the coconut. Press the mixture over the base of the prepared pan in an even thickness. Refrigerate until firm.

3 In a frying pan over low heat, stir the strawberries, brown sugar, and balsamic vinegar until the strawberries release their juice, then allow to simmer until the sauce starts to thicken. Pour the strawberries into a colander over a large bowl and gently press on the fruit to extract the juice. Leave the strawberries to drain in the colander until cool, then pour the sauce into a bowl, cover and refrigerate until ready to serve.

4 In a large bowl and using electric beaters, beat the cream cheese until smooth, then add the confectioners' sugar and beat again. Add the mascarpone and strawberry solids left in the colander and stir until fully incorporated. Spread the cream cheese mixture over the hardened chocolate base and refrigerate overnight, or until firm.

5 To serve, run a knife around the edge of the cheesecake, then release the side of the pan. Gently slide the cheesecake onto a serving plate, removing the parchment paper as you go. Decorate the top with whipped cream if you like, cut cake into wedges, and serve drizzled with the strawberry sauce.

Serves 8–10

Fruit tarts

½ quantity **Sweet short-crust pastry**
  (recipe page 170)

Pastry cream
1 cup whipping cream
1 cup milk
½ cup superfine sugar
2 eggs
⅓ cup cornstarch
½ teaspoon vanilla extract
1 oz (2 tablespoons) butter, cut into
    four cubes
mixed berries and sliced strawberries,
    to serve

1 Grease six 3¼-inch individual tart pans (or one 9½-inch round tart pan).

2 Roll out the pastry between two sheets of parchment paper into a large circle, then turn the pastry over to smooth any creases on the back. Remove the top sheet of parchment paper and cut out four 4½-inch circles. Ease the pastry into the pans, then cut off any excess pastry by pressing a rolling pin over the top edge of the pans. Re-roll the leftover pastry scraps to make two more circles. Patch any holes with pastry off-cuts. Refrigerate for at least 1 hour.

3 Preheat the oven to 325°F. Prick the pastry cases a few times with a skewer and place onto a baking sheet. Bake for 10 minutes, then reduce the oven to 315°F and bake for another 10–15 minutes until lightly browned. Remove the pans from the oven and cool to room temperature.

4 To make the pastry cream, place the cream, milk, and sugar into a saucepan and stir over low heat until the sugar has dissolved, then leave to simmer until bubbles just start to appear around the side of the saucepan.

5 In a heatproof bowl, whisk the eggs to combine, then whisk in the cornstarch until smooth. Slowly pour the warm cream mixture into the eggs, whisking constantly. Return to the saucepan and whisk continuously over low heat until thickened. (If necessary, use a hand-held blender to remove any lumps.) Remove the pan from the heat and whisk in the vanilla and then the butter, one piece at a time, until incorporated. Cover closely with plastic wrap to prevent a skin forming and set aside to cool, or refrigerate until needed.

6 Gently remove the pastry cases from their pans, fill generously with the fully cooled custard, and decorate the top with berries and sliced strawberries. Refrigerate for at least 1 hour before serving.

Makes 6 individual tarts or 1 large tart, which serves 8

Baked maple custards with pecan praline

3 eggs
2 egg yolks
1 cup whipping cream
1 cup milk
1 cup pure maple syrup
½ teaspoon vanilla extract
pinch of salt

Pecan praline
½ cup superfine sugar
½ cup pecan nuts, toasted

1 Preheat the oven to 315°F. Place six 4 fl oz/½ cup ramekins into a large baking dish. Boil some water.

2 In a blender, put the eggs, egg yolks, cream, milk, maple syrup, vanilla, and salt. Blend until smooth, then pour into the ramekins. Place the baking dish into the oven and pour enough boiling water around the ramekins to come halfway up the sides.

3 Bake the custards for 35–45 minutes, or until set, then carefully remove the ramekins to a wire rack to cool. Cover with plastic wrap and refrigerate overnight.

4 Line a baking sheet with parchment paper. To make the pecan praline, combine the sugar and 2 tablespoons water in a small saucepan. Stir over low heat until the sugar dissolves, then increase the heat and boil, without stirring, until the syrup turns a deep amber color. Immediately remove the pan from the heat and add the pecans, swirl the pan to combine, then pour the toffee onto the prepared baking sheet and cool until set. Break the praline into pieces and process in a food processor until finely ground. Place into an airtight container and set aside.

5 To serve, remove the custards from the refrigerator 10 minutes before required. Before serving, sprinkle with pecan praline.

Serves 6

Sponge flan with coconut cream custard

In this recipe I use a recessed sponge pan (maryann cake pan) with a fluted edge and an indented bottom, so that when the cooked cake is flipped over you have a perfect shell to fill.

1 recipe **Genoise sponge cake** batter
    (recipe page 143)

Coconut cream custard
1½ cups coconut cream
¼ teaspoon vanilla extract
4 large egg yolks
¼ cup superfine sugar
1 tablespoon cornstarch

To serve
confectioners' sugar, sifted
1⅔ cups strawberries, puréed

1 To make the coconut cream custard, put the coconut cream and vanilla in a saucepan and bring to a simmer.

2 In a heatproof bowl, beat the egg yolks, superfine sugar, and cornstarch together until very thick and pale, then pour in the warm coconut cream and beat slowly until incorporated. Return the mixture to the saucepan and cook over medium heat, whisking until boiling and thickened. Cover and refrigerate until needed.

3 Preheat the oven to 350°F, positioning the rack in the lower third of the oven. Grease and line the raised base of a maryann pan with parchment paper.

4 Follow the method to make the Genoise sponge cake batter, then pour the batter into the prepared pan and bake for 12–15 minutes, or until evenly browned and pulling away from the side, turning the pan around after 8 minutes. Remove from the oven and allow the cake to firm up in the pan for 10 minutes, then turn out onto a wire rack and gently remove the parchment paper. Flip the cake over to cool on the flat base.

5 When the shell is fully cooled, sprinkle the edge with confectioners' sugar and fill the cavity with cold coconut cream custard. To serve, cut into slices and serve drizzled with a little strawberry purée.

Serves 8

Sticky rice with tropical fruit salad

1 cup glutinous rice, soaked overnight in
   3 cups water
1½ cups coconut milk
2 tablespoons superfine sugar
pinch of salt
1 large mango
½ small red papaya
12 lychees
½ small pineapple

1 Line a steamer basket with parchment paper and poke a few holes in the paper with a skewer.

2 Drain the rice, put it into the steamer basket, and cover with the lid. Set the basket over simmering water in a large pan or wok and steam for about 15 minutes, or until the rice is translucent.

3 While the rice is cooking, simmer the coconut milk, sugar, and a pinch of salt in a small saucepan, stirring until the sugar is dissolved.

4 Peel, remove the seeds, and chop all the fruit into small pieces and mix together in a bowl.

5 Place the cooked rice into a heatproof bowl, pour over 1 cup of the hot coconut milk, and stir only until just mixed. Set aside briefly until absorbed. If left for too long, the cooled rice tends to set into a fairly solid block, so don't start this step too far ahead.

6 To serve, spoon a little of the sticky rice into dessert bowls, drizzle with the remaining warm coconut milk, and top with some of the tropical fruit salad.

Serves 6

Lime and coconut tart

I'm sure silicone bakeware was invented just for gluten-free baked goods, which are often very difficult to remove from regular baking pans. A silicone tart pan or liner is perfect for this recipe with its macaroon-style crust, or failing that a straight-sided, loose-based pan makes removing the finished tart much easier than a typical tart pan with a fluted edge.

⅓ cup superfine sugar
1 egg, separated
1½ cups desiccated coconut,
    unsweetened

Lime curd
6 egg yolks
¾ cup sugar
1 tablespoon finely grated lime zest
1 tablespoon lime juice
2 tablespoons lemon juice
4½ oz (9 tablespoons) butter, chopped

1 Preheat the oven to 315°F. Use a 9-inch round silicone tart pan or grease a regular non-stick tart pan with a removable base and line the base with parchment paper.

2 In a bowl, stir the sugar and egg yolk until combined, then stir in the coconut and mix well. In a glass or stainless-steel bowl, beat the egg white to firm peak stage. Fold the egg white into the coconut mixture and mix gently until fully incorporated.

3 Using wet fingers, press the coconut mixture over the base and side of the tart pan, ensuring there is a consistent thickness, especially on the sides — any thick spots will be hard to cut. Bake for about 10 minutes, or until evenly browned, then allow to cool to room temperature before filling.

4 To make the lime curd, put the egg yolks, sugar, lime zest, lime juice, and lemon juice into the top of a double boiler over gently simmering water. Whisk constantly for about 10 minutes, or until very thick and a pale lemon color. It's important not to shortcut this step or the curd won't set properly.

5 Remove the pan from the heat and add the butter one piece at a time, whisking constantly until fully incorporated. Cover the curd closely with plastic wrap and set aside to cool to room temperature. When cooled, spoon the curd into the prepared shell and refrigerate until set.

6 To serve, carefully remove the tart from the pan, cut into wedges, and serve plain or with a scoop of **Vanilla-bean ice cream** (recipe page 148).

Serves 8

Tiramisu trifle

1 recipe **Genoise sponge cake**
   (recipe page 143)
6 egg yolks
¼ cup superfine sugar
2¼ cups mascarpone cheese
5 fl oz heavy cream
4 fl oz (½ cup) Kahlúa
4 fl oz (½ cup) strong brewed coffee
finely grated chocolate, to decorate

1 Bake the Genoise sponge cake in two 8-inch round cake pans, then allow to cool to room temperature.

2 Place some ice cubes into a bowl large enough to hold your heatproof mixing bowl.

3 In a heatproof bowl over gently simmering water, whisk the egg yolks and sugar until very thick and pale. This takes about 10 minutes and ensures the egg yolks are cooked, however you will need to whisk constantly or you will end up with sweet scrambled eggs!

4 Remove the bowl from the heat, stand it in the larger bowl with the ice cubes and continue whisking until the custard has cooled to room temperature. Add the mascarpone and cream to the custard and whisk until smooth. Cover and refrigerate until the custard has thickened to a spreading consistency.

5 In a separate bowl, combine the Kahlúa and coffee.

6 Split both the cakes in half horizontally and lay on a cutting board, cut side up. Brush each one generously with the Kahlúa and coffee mixture, then place one piece into the base of a glass bowl. Spread one quarter of the mascarpone custard on top, cover with another piece of cake, and repeat the process to finish with a layer of custard. Sprinkle the top with grated chocolate, cover the bowl and refrigerate for at least 4 hours, or preferably overnight to allow the flavors to develop.

7 Serve with any leftover Kahlúa and coffee mixture.

Serves 8

BASICS

On the following pages you will find a few of those handy recipes that are used over and over.

Chicken broth

I use this broth in lots of recipes, including soups, risottos, and stews, so I always like to have some frozen in portions in the freezer.

1 lb 8 oz chicken necks
2 carrots, diced
1 white onion, diced
1 celery stalk, diced
1 teaspoon crushed garlic
1 tablespoon olive oil
1 cup white wine
6 parsley sprigs
1 teaspoon peppercorns
2 bay leaves, broken

1 In a large stockpot, sauté the chicken necks, carrots, onion, celery, and garlic in the olive oil until well browned. Pour in the wine and stir to scrape up the brown residue on the bottom of the pot.

2 Add 6 cups water, parsley, peppercorns, and bay leaves, then cover and bring to a boil. Reduce the heat and simmer the stock for 2 hours, skimming the surface if necessary. Strain into a large bowl, discard the solids, and refrigerate until needed. Discard any fat that has solidified on the top. Freeze for up to 3 months.

Makes about 6 cups

Sweet and sour sauce

I always have some of this sauce in the freezer for nights when I don't feel like cooking. It's a great sauce to have on standby for tossing through stir-fried vegetables, pork, or shrimp.

1 cup pineapple juice
2 tablespoons brown sugar
2 tablespoons tomato paste
    (concentrated purée)
1 tablespoon rice vinegar
1 tablespoon oyster sauce*
1 teaspoon soy sauce*
1 teaspoon fish sauce*
juice of ½ lime
2 teaspoons cornstarch

1 Combine the pineapple juice, sugar, tomato paste, vinegar, oyster sauce, soy sauce, fish sauce, and lime juice in a saucepan. Bring to a boil over medium heat, then reduce the heat to a simmer.

2 In a small bowl, make a slurry with the cornstarch and 2 tablespoons water, then add this to the sauce and stir until it starts to thicken. Continue stirring over low heat for another 1–2 minutes. Allow the sauce to cool, then cover and refrigerate overnight or for up to 1 week, or freeze in portions.

Makes 1½ cups

White sauce

White sauce will form a skin if made too far ahead or stored in the fridge, so cover closely with plastic wrap, then remove the wrap and whisk while reheating.

2¼ oz (4½ tablespoons) butter
2 tablespoons cornstarch
2 cups milk
salt, to taste

Optional additions
❋ ½ teaspoon French or whole grain mustard* (I always add French mustard)
❋ ¼ cup grated parmesan or jarlsberg cheese
❋ 1 handful chopped flat-leaf (Italian) parsley

1 Melt the butter in a small saucepan over medium heat, then remove the pan from the stove. Add the cornstarch and whisk to combine, then return the pan to the heat for 1–2 minutes.

2 Slowly pour in the milk, whisking continuously, then continue to whisk until the sauce begins to boil and thicken. Add the mustard, cheese or herbs, if using, then season with salt to taste. Reduce the heat to very low and simmer for a few minutes. Serve hot.

Makes about 2 cups

Chimichurri

This is my version of chimichurri, a condiment popular in South America where small bowls are placed on the table beside the salt and pepper.

2 large handfuls flat-leaf (Italian) parsley
1 handful cilantro leaves
1 small scallion, white part only
¼ teaspoon crushed garlic
2 teaspoons white wine vinegar or lemon juice
generous pinch of salt
¼ cup olive oil
freshly ground black pepper
chili flakes, to taste

1 Place the herbs, scallion, garlic, vinegar or lemon juice, and a generous pinch of salt into the bowl of a food processor and process until roughly chopped, stopping a few times to scrape down the side of the bowl.

2 Pour in the olive oil and process again until the herbs are very finely chopped. Season to taste with extra salt, freshly ground black pepper, and chili flakes. Store covered in the refrigerator for up to 5 days. Serve at room temperature.

Makes ⅓ cup

Potato pastry

This is the pastry I use for savory dishes such as baked samosas, pasties, calzones, and Sausage rolls (recipe page 40).

1 cup **Rice flour blend** (recipe page 9)
½ teaspoon baking powder
½ teaspoon salt
3½ oz (7 tablespoons) chilled butter, cubed
7 oz cold mashed potato (mashed without butter or milk)

1 Put the Rice flour blend, baking powder, and salt in the bowl of a food processor and pulse to combine. Add the butter and pulse to form even-sized crumbs. Add the potato and pulse only until the dough starts to come together.

2 Turn out onto a large sheet of parchment paper and knead briefly to form a smooth ball. Cut in half and flatten each one a little, then cover with plastic wrap and refrigerate for at least 30 minutes (or up to 3 days). Remove the pastry from the refrigerator and allow to soften a little before rolling out.

Makes 1 quantity

Sweet short-crust pastry

I used to be intimidated by pastry, but this recipe is so easy — I whizz it up in the food processor without a second thought.

1½ cups **Rice flour blend** (recipe page 9)
⅓ cup confectioners' sugar
1 teaspoon xanthan gum
3½ oz (7 tablespoons) butter, softened
4½ oz cream cheese, softened
1 egg yolk
1 teaspoon vanilla extract

1 Combine the Rice flour blend, confectioners' sugar, and xanthan gum in a bowl.

2 Place the butter, cream cheese, egg yolk, and vanilla into the bowl of a food processor and process until smooth. Add the dry ingredients and pulse only until the dough starts to form a ball. Remove the dough to a large sheet of parchment paper, knead to form a smooth ball, then divide in half and flatten into two discs. Cover each disc closely with plastic wrap and chill for at least 1 hour or up to 2 days

Makes 1 quantity

Jaffa blackout

This is a quick but decadent dessert sauce.

6 oz dark chocolate, broken into pieces
1 cup heavy whipping cream
1 tablespoon light corn syrup
1 tablespoon orange liqueur, such as
    Cointreau
1 teaspoon very finely chopped
    orange zest

1 Place the chocolate, cream, and corn syrup into the top of a double boiler over gently simmering water and stir until the chocolate has melted and the sauce is smooth.

2 Remove the pan from the heat and stir in the liqueur. Serve the sauce warm drizzled over your favorite dessert and sprinkle lightly with orange zest.

Makes about 1$\frac{1}{2}$ cups

Sundae sauce

Spooned over Vanilla-bean ice cream (recipe page 148) and topped with chopped macadamia nuts and grated chocolate, this makes a perfect treat any day of the week.

¾ cup light corn syrup
½ cup superfine sugar
½ cup cranberry juice or water
2 egg whites
few drops red food color (optional)
few drops rosewater (optional)

1 In a saucepan, combine the corn syrup, sugar, and juice and stir to dissolve the sugar. Place the uncovered pan over high heat and bring to a boil. When the entire surface is boiling rapidly, set a timer for 5 minutes.

2 While the syrup boils, beat the egg whites to firm peak stage. Once the timer has rung, gently pour the syrup down the side of the bowl into the egg whites, beating all the time, until the syrup is fully incorporated.

3 Add a few drops of red food coloring for a deeper shade of pink and a few drops of rosewater to taste, if desired.

Makes about 3 cups

Index

Acknowledgments

Once again I'm indebted to Stephanie Alexander, who sat so patiently on the kitchen bench and answered all my culinary queries, simply and quickly.

Thank you also to my wonderful husband who works as my kitchen hand, storeman and packer, computer wizard, delivery boy and technical advisor (here try this, now try this one), when he's not flying 747s around the world. To the very clever Libby Ginn, whose stunning photos once again illustrate my recipes, and whose company as always made our shooting days a pleasure. Many thanks Lib!

Thank you to my cheery agent Tara Wynne at Curtis Brown for not calling security when I cornered her at a writer's center event, and for her timely introduction to Kay Scarlett and the team at Murdoch Books.

Since publishing my first book I've been overwhelmed by the warm personal responses I have received. So many people took the time to write or email with their appreciation, and I just wanted to say how touched I was by their thoughtfulness. This positive feedback gave me so much more confidence as I approached my second book, and their suggestions and requests helped guide my selection of food and recipes.

Thank you also to the many independent retailers who showed great faith in me in the early days and for their continued support and encouragement, especially the staff at Wheel&Barrow stores around Australia.

I've been very lucky and am truly grateful. RR